Beyond the Bleachers

How to Raise the Athlete Without Losing the Child

Walter A. Beede

I0617473

Contents

Part I — The New Reality of Youth Sports

Chapter 1: Youth Sports Changed

Why Parents Feel Overwhelmed, Anxious, and Behind
I remember when youth sports still felt local.

You played close to home. You knew the coaches — they were your neighbors, the dad two streets over, the math teacher who ran the rec league on Saturdays. The field belonged to the community, not to a business model. Families gathered on a Saturday morning because they loved the game and loved watching their children play, and when it was over everybody went to get pancakes. Nobody was ranked. Nobody was filmed. Nobody drove four hours to prove anything.

I am old enough to have watched that world quietly disappear, and I have watched it from every seat there is — as an athlete, as a college head coach evaluating talent, as an advisor sitting across the kitchen table from frightened families, and as a father in the middle of it myself. From each of those seats the view is different, and parents usually only get to see one. So let me tell you what it looks like from all of them at once: the game your child plays is still good. The world around the game changed, and it changed in a direction that runs on your fear.

Here is the shift in one sentence. Parents used to ask, "Is my athlete having fun?" Now they ask, "Are we falling behind?"

That question — are we behind — is the engine of this entire book, because it is the question that every part of the modern youth sports machine is designed to plant in your chest and keep there. And it works. It works on

smart parents, loving parents, parents who swore they would never be "that parent." It works because it attaches itself to the thing you care about most.

What actually changed

Walk through what a family is asked to navigate today that simply did not exist a generation ago. Travel teams. Club programs. Private trainers. Ranking services. Recruiting platforms. Social media profiles. Showcases. Combines. Specialty camps. Year-round schedules. Strength coaches. Position-specific instructors. Tournament weekends in cities you had to map. Hotel blocks. Highlight videos. Team group chats that never go quiet. Online comparison running twenty-four hours a day. Exposure promises from people who profit when you believe them.

Each of those things can have real value at the right time for the right athlete. Stacked together and aimed at a nine-year-old, they become a pressure system. And the money is real now in a way it never was. Families spend an average of over a thousand dollars a year on a single child's primary sport — and for the travel-and-showcase families, several times that. That spending has climbed nearly fifty percent in just a few years, far faster than the cost of ordinary life. So the stakes feel higher because, financially, they are.

But the deepest change isn't the money or the calendar. It's the volume. Everywhere a parent turns, a different voice says the same four things in a different accent:

Do not fall behind. Do not miss this opportunity. Do not let another athlete pass yours. Do not say no.

You cannot escape it. It's in the bleachers, in the parking lot, in the group chat, in the algorithm, in the flyer taped to the gym door. And when a message is everywhere, it stops feeling like marketing and starts feeling like truth.

Why it lands so hard on good parents

Here's what I want you to understand, because it will take the shame off your shoulders: feeling overwhelmed by this does not make you weak or foolish. It makes you a normal parent who loves a child in an abnormal environment.

The pressure works precisely because you're a good parent. A parent who didn't care wouldn't feel it. The fear of "falling behind" only has teeth

because you would do anything for your athlete and the machine knows it. So it sells you the one thing no loving parent can easily refuse: insurance against being the reason your child missed out.

I've sat with hundreds of these families. The dad who's spent twenty thousand dollars and can't tell you what his son actually got better at. The mom refreshing a stat app every half inning while her daughter looks up into the stands for a face that isn't watching the game, only the numbers. The family that hasn't had a free Saturday in three years and can't remember deciding to give them up — it happened one reasonable "yes" at a time. None of them are bad parents. Every one of them got swept into a current they didn't see until they were already in it.

What this book is not, and what it is

This book is not an attack on youth sports. It is not an attack on coaches, trainers, clubs, showcases, or travel teams. There are extraordinary people in this space — coaches who change lives, programs that build athletes the right way, trainers who understand age and stage and the whole human being, events that open real doors at the right moment for the right athlete. I've spent my life among them. The good ones are worth everything.

But there is also a great deal of fear being sold to families, and when good parents are afraid, they start chasing. And chasing — not the sport itself — is what damages athletes, drains families, and quietly kills the joy that made an athlete fall in love with the game in the first place.

So here is what I believe you need to hear before anything else in this book:

You do not have to let fear make the plan. You do not have to chase everything. You do not have to buy every opportunity. You do not have to turn your child's childhood into a ten-year audition. You do not have to let another family's calendar become your family's plan. You do not have to sacrifice the athlete, the family, or the joy to prove you are committed.

The world around youth sports changed. Your job did not. Your job is still to raise a healthy, whole human being who happens to play a sport — and to protect the part of the game that was always worth protecting: a child, moving, competing, failing, recovering, belonging, and coming back the next day because they love it.

The chapters ahead give you the framework to do that without drowning. We start by naming the thing in the water.

Chapter Tool

Parent Reflection: What Has Changed Since I Played?

Use this before you make another sports decision. Write short, honest answers.

1. What did youth sports feel like when I was young?

2. What feels different now for my athlete?

3. What pressure am I carrying that my athlete may not even understand?

4. Am I making decisions from the child in front of me, or from the system around me?

5. What part of the game do I most want to protect for my athlete?

Parent reset: The game may have changed. My job has not. I am here to support the athlete, protect the family, and keep the long game in focus.

Chapter 2: The Business of Anxiety

How Fear Became the Most Profitable Emotion in Youth Sports

Let me tell you the most honest thing I know about the business I've spent my life inside, and I'll say it plainly, because it took me years on the inside to see it clearly:

The youth sports industry does not always sell development first. Too often, it sells uncertainty.

It sells the feeling that another family knows something you don't. It sells the suspicion that someone, somewhere, is doing more for their child than you're doing for yours. It sells the belief that one missed team, one missed camp, one missed showcase, one missed trainer, one missed weekend could be the thing that changes everything.

That is how fear becomes a business model. And once you see the model, you can't unsee it — which is exactly why I want to show it to you now, before you spend another dollar.

Why fear is the perfect product

Think for a moment about what fear does to a buyer.

A calm, grounded customer is a terrible customer for this industry. They ask hard questions. They compare value. They sleep on it. They say "not this year" and walk away without flinching. You cannot build a predictable business on a customer like that.

A frightened customer is the dream. A frightened parent spends faster, travels farther, asks fewer questions, accepts more pressure, signs up sooner, and overlooks more warning signs. Not because they're foolish — because they love their child and cannot bear the thought of being the reason an opportunity slipped away. Fear quiets the part of the mind that evaluates and hands the wallet straight to the part that protects. That is a marketer's dream, and the people selling to you know it better than you do.

So if you set out to build a business in this space and you wanted reliable revenue, you would not actually lead with the best training. The best training is slow, quiet, and honest, and it's a hard thing to sell. You would lead with the fear of falling behind. It never runs out. It scales without limit. And it closes the sale every single time.

I'm not telling you everyone in youth sports is cynical. Most aren't — there are extraordinary, devoted people in this world, and I've spent my life among them. But the incentives of the industry reward fear, and over time incentives beat intentions. The flyer that whispers "limited spots — secure your child's future today" will always outperform the one that says "good coaching, sane schedule, come when it fits your family." Fear is simply the better advertisement. That is the quiet tragedy of the whole enterprise.

But here is the part the industry can't do alone

Now I have to say the harder half of this, the half that most books in this aisle leave out — because it's the half that isn't comfortable.

The industry can sell fear all day long. But somebody still has to buy it.

And that somebody is us. The parents.

No showcase company can take your money without your hand reaching for the card. No ranking service can rattle you without you choosing to open the app and look. No flyer, no email, no confident parent in the group chat can make the decision for you. The machine is real, and it is aimed directly at your love — but it has no power until the fear it's selling meets a fear that's already living in you, ready to be activated. The sale only closes because, somewhere inside, we were already afraid.

I know this because I have been the buyer. I have felt that stomach-drop when another family announced the thing we hadn't done. I have reached for the "solution" — the extra event, the next lesson — not because I'd thought it through, but because the fear needed quieting and spending money quieted it for an afternoon. I'm not describing a foolish parent I once met. I'm describing the man I had to learn not to be.

So yes — be angry at the industry that preys on your love. That anger is earned. But understand that anger at the machine, by itself, will not protect your child. Because the machine isn't the thing making the final decision in your kitchen at ten o'clock at night. You are. The salesman can knock all day. You're still the one who decides whether to open the door.

That is not bad news. It's the best news in this book. Because it means the one variable you can't control — the industry — was never the one that mattered most. The one that matters most is the one sitting in your own chest. And that one, you can learn to govern.

What fear builds when you let it

Here's what's at stake if you don't.

Fear is a terrible architect. Hand it the blueprints for a childhood and watch what it builds: calendars with no white space. Schedules heavier than most adults could carry. Expectations far too grown-up for a child still learning who they are. A second team because the first wasn't enough. A trainer because the neighbor hired one. A showcase three states away because an email said this might be the one. A year-round grind in a single sport at the exact age a body and a heart most need variety and rest.

No single one of those decisions looks crazy. Each is a reasonable answer to a frightening question. But stack them up, year over year, all built by fear — and you get the exhausted, joyless, over-scheduled young athlete I have met a thousand times. Busy fifty weeks a year and somehow getting worse: more tired, more anxious, less in love with the game every season.

Fear never means to build that. Fear just answers every question with the same word — more — and more compounds into a childhood nobody actually chose.

The two questions

I can usually tell within five minutes of meeting a family which engine is driving them, because it shows up in the question they ask.

A grounded parent asks: What does my child actually need?

A frightened parent asks: What if we miss out?

The two sound almost identical, and both come from love. But they build completely different childhoods. The first starts with the real child in front of you — their stage, their body, their joy, their readiness. It produces decisions that fit. The second starts with an imagined rival and an imagined closing door. It produces decisions that chase.

One builds an athlete. The other builds a customer. And the entire industry is engineered to keep you asking the second question — because the second question always has something to sell you, and the first one usually doesn't.

Taking the engine back

You reclaim your power the moment you can catch the fear in the act.

When the flyer tightens your stomach. When the group chat makes your hand drift toward your wallet. When the email says the door is closing. In that exact moment, stop and ask yourself one plain question: Is this my child's actual need talking — or is it my fear?

Because fear is a feeling, not a fact. It arrives dressed as urgent truth, but most of the time it's just the most profitable emotion in youth sports, doing the job it was sold to do on you. You are allowed to feel it completely and still refuse to obey it.

The families who do best over the long haul aren't the fearless ones — nobody's fearless about their own child. They're the ones who learned to recognize the fear, name it out loud, and refuse to let it hold the pen.

The train that is not arriving yet

One of the cleanest ways to catch fear-based advice is to listen for a voice trying to make an eleven- or twelve-year-old's decision sound like a college door swinging shut.

If someone tells you your young child is about to miss a train that won't pull into the station for six or seven years, ask them for next week's lottery numbers while they're at it.

This isn't to say preparation doesn't matter — it matters deeply. But panic is not preparation. The young years are for building foundation, skill, coordination, confidence, love of the game, academic habits, body awareness, and healthy relationships with coaches and teammates. They are not to be run like a countdown clock toward a recruiting date that's still years over the horizon.

A trusted voice creates clarity. A fear-based voice creates urgency. Learn to tell them apart, and you've already taken back half your power.

Temporary headlines, permanent decisions

One more form of anxiety earns its own warning: the temporary headline.

Every few months the youth sports world serves up a fresh one. A rule proposal. An eligibility rumor. A recruiting-calendar tweak. A transfer story. A social media thread that leaves every parent feeling as if the ground shifted under their child overnight.

Do not make a permanent decision from a temporary headline.

A headline may matter. A rule may eventually matter. Stay informed — but informed is not the same as panicked. A headline should never push a family to repeat a grade, abandon a school, rewrite an academic path, chase an academy, skip a season, or redraw a child's life before the facts are final and before anyone's confirmed the rule even applies to their child's level.

Here's the pattern, every time: the eligibility question is for the few. The anxiety is sold to everybody. A narrow rule discussion becomes a broad panic. A Division I issue becomes a middle-school crisis. A proposal becomes a decision. A rumor becomes an invoice.

Slow down. Ask what's actually final. Ask what level it applies to. Ask whether it changes the real work in front of you. Almost always, it won't — because the work in front of you is still the work: build the athlete, build the transcript, protect the joy, prepare the body, protect the family, and decide from truth instead of fear.

The industry will keep selling the fear. That part is out of your hands. Whether you keep buying it is not.

Chapter 3: I Will Not Let Fear Make the Plan

You already know the question. You've just never said it where anyone could hear you.

It comes at night, usually. The house is quiet, the gear bag is by the door for tomorrow, and you're lying there doing math you'd never admit to doing — the money, the years, the other kid who got the offer, the ranking that came out Tuesday. And underneath all of it is the question you would never ask out loud at the team dinner, because asking it would mean admitting you've been thinking it:

Is my kid actually good enough? And if they are not — did I fail them? Did I miss something? Did I not do enough?

I've spent thirty years around this game, on every side of it, and I'm going to tell you something most people in youth sports will never tell you, because their living depends on you not hearing it.

That fear you feel? The industry didn't put it there. It just found it.

The travel team, the showcase, the ranking service, the trainer with the waitlist — none of them can sell fear to a parent who isn't already afraid. They're not creating the panic. They're billing you for it. And the reason their pitch lands, every time, is that it speaks directly to a thing that was already alive in you before you ever heard of them. So before we talk about them, we have to talk about you. The hardest truth is that some of this is coming from inside the house.

The fear isn't about your kid

I'm not standing above you when I say this. I have been the father in the seat. I have felt the fear in my own chest. I have wanted the outcome — wanted it badly, wanted it for reasons that were about me as much as about my child. I've had to learn, sometimes the hard way, that love and control are not the same thing. So when I name these things, understand I'm naming my own.

Here's the part that's going to sting, and I need you to sit in it instead of flinching away.

When you lie awake afraid your child is falling behind, you tell yourself it's for them. It feels like love. It feels like the most selfless thing in the world — you'd do anything for this kid. But be honest with me the way you can't be honest at the field: a good portion of that fear isn't about your child at all.

It's about you.

It's the fear of being the parent who didn't do enough — who'll have to look at a kid at eighteen and wonder if one skipped showcase cost them everything. It's the fear of what the other families think when you're the one who said no. It's the quiet, unbearable possibility that your kid simply isn't as special as you needed them to be — and the way that lands on you, on your genes, your effort, your worth as their parent. And for some of us — and I'm including the man I used to be in this — it's a dream that started as theirs and slowly, without our ever deciding it, became ours.

I'm not telling you this to shame you. Shame is useless; it just makes people defensive, and a defensive parent can't change. I'm telling you because you cannot put down a weight you refuse to admit you're carrying. And until you can name what you're actually afraid of, you will keep handing that weight to a child who never asked to carry it.

The things we do and hope no one notices

Let me say the quiet parts out loud. Not to indict you — to free you. Because every one of these is something I've either done myself or watched a thousand loving parents do, and not one of us would say it at the dinner table.

You check the ranking app before you check on your kid.

You tell everyone it's about their love of the game, but you know exactly what their stat line was last weekend and you're not sure you could name a single thing that made them laugh.

You are warmer to your child after a good game than after a bad one. You know you do it. You've told yourself you don't, and you do, and your kid clocked it years ago.

There's a version of your own athletic story — the one that ended too soon, the one where you wonder what might have been — and somewhere in here you've quietly assigned your child the job of finishing it for you.

You've watched the joy drain out of your kid over the last two seasons and you've kept going anyway, because stopping would mean admitting that all of it — the money, the weekends, the identity you built as the parent of the athlete — was spent on something that might already be over.

If even one of those landed, you're not a bad parent. You're a normal one, caught in a machine built by people who understand your love better than you do and aim at it on purpose. But you felt that flinch of recognition for a reason. That flinch is the most useful thing that's happened to you in this whole book. Don't run from it. That's the door.

What the fear does to the one you're trying to protect

Here's the cruelest part of all of it, and the reason I won't soften this chapter. Your child can feel everything you think you're hiding.

They can feel the difference between a parent watching them and a parent measuring them. They can find your face in a crowd of three hundred people and read, in half a second, whether you're delighted they exist or auditing them for evidence. When you turn the car ride home into a performance review — even a gentle one, even a "just trying to help" one — you are not correcting their footwork. You are teaching them that your warmth has conditions, and that the condition is winning.

And once a kid believes they are being measured instead of loved, you have taken away the one thing they needed most from you and could get nowhere else: a place to rest. Score twenty, and someone scored twenty-four. Make the team, and someone made the better one. There is no number high enough to finally earn them home, because you've quietly turned home into one more place they're being evaluated. They will spend the rest of their childhood — and a frightening number of them, the rest of their adult lives — trying to perform their way into a love they should have gotten for free.

That is what fear builds when you let it hold the pen. Not a more committed athlete. A child who learns that they are only as valuable as their last result, and a parent who can't understand, years later, why the kid won't call.

Why "calm down" is going to cost you something

Now — here's where most books in this aisle would put their arm around you and say relax, you're not behind, slow down, protect the joy. And all of that is true. But I refuse to hand it to you for free, because easy reassurance is part of what keeps parents stuck.

Choosing not to let fear make the plan is going to cost you something real, and you should know the price before you agree to it.

It may cost you a kid who is less successful than they could have been. That's the trade nobody says out loud. You can probably squeeze another ten percent out of your child — more reps, more pressure, more showcases, less rest, less childhood. It might even work. But the cost of that last ten percent is frequently a kid who burns out, gets hurt, or quietly comes to hate the thing they once loved and the parent who pushed it. So you have to decide, on purpose, eyes open: are you willing to let your child be good instead of maximized, if maximized means losing them? That is not a comfortable sentence. I'm not going to pretend it is.

It will cost you the approval of the other families — the ones who will drive three states away, who will sign up for the thing you skipped, who will look at your "no" as a lack of commitment. You have to be willing to be misunderstood by people whose own fear you've decided not to share.

And it will cost you the dream, at least the version of it you were holding. Because letting fear go means letting the outcome go — means raising a child whose future is genuinely theirs to win or lose or walk away from, not a project you get to manage to a result. That's a kind of grief. Real love usually is.

If your version of "calming down" costs you nothing, it isn't the real thing. It's just a more relaxed way of staying afraid.

The sentence, and what it actually demands

So here is the sentence I want you to carry into every season, every invoice, every car ride, every 10:45 p.m. group chat that makes your stomach drop:
I will not let fear make the plan.

But understand what you're actually promising when you say it. You are not promising to care less. You are promising something much harder. You're promising to feel the fear — fully, because you will — and then refuse to obey it. You're promising that your child will not be handed your anxiety to carry. You're promising that when the moment comes to choose between your ego and their childhood, between the dream you're holding and the kid actually standing in front of you, you'll choose the kid. Not once, when it's easy. Every time, especially when it costs you.

That promise will ask you to look smaller than the loud parents. It will ask you to spend less and trust more. It will ask you to love a child you cannot control, headed toward a future you cannot guarantee, and to find that enough.

It is the hardest thing this book will ask of you. It is also the only thing that was ever going to work.

So tonight, when the house is quiet and the gear bag is by the door and the math starts up again in the dark — don't reach for the credit card, the trainer, the next thing that promises to quiet the fear. Sit with the real question instead. Not is my kid good enough.

Am I about to make this decision from love — or from fear wearing love's clothes?

You already know the difference. You always did. The only question that was ever on the table is whether you'll have the courage to act on the answer.

Chapter 4: The Resource You Cannot Replace

Time, Childhood, Family, and the True Cost of Chasing

Every invoice in youth sports shows you a number. None of them show you the real price.

The entry fee, the team dues, the trainer's hourly rate, the hotel block, the tournament registration — those are the visible costs, and parents agonize over them. But the most expensive thing youth sports will ever ask of your family doesn't appear on any invoice, and once it's spent, no scholarship, no ranking, and no trophy will ever buy it back.

The real cost is time you cannot replace — the finite, non-refundable hours of a childhood and a family. So before we go any further, let me give you

the short list of things a family should never sacrifice for youth sports, because a family that protects this list can chase excellence all day long without ever losing the thing that actually matters. Cross these lines, and the trophies won't cover the cost.

The relationship. You will have your athlete for life. They will have the sport for a few years. Never trade the lifetime thing for the temporary thing. I have watched families win the season and lose the relationship — athletes who made it to the next level and could barely stand to call home, because somewhere along the way Mom or Dad stopped being a parent and became a manager, a critic, a performance reviewer in the passenger seat. If the sport is damaging how your athlete feels about you, the sport is too expensive at any price. There is no banner worth that trade.

The athlete's mental and physical health. No game, no ranking, no scholarship is worth a body run into the ground or a spirit quietly broken. Health is the floor of everything, and you do not negotiate the floor. The over-trained, under-rested, chronically hurt young athlete is one of the most common products of fear-based chasing, and the damage — to growth plates, to joints, to the relationship with their own body — can last decades. Protect the health first. Everything else is built on top of it.

Childhood itself. This is the one parents grieve most, and always too late. The unstructured, un-filmed, un-coached part of being young — the free Saturday, the bike ride to nowhere, the afternoon of being gloriously bored in the backyard, the sleepover, the pickup game with no adults and no score kept. You cannot buy that back later. I have sat with more families than I can count who chased hard for ten years, and a stunning number of them say the same quiet thing: they wish they'd kept some of the ordinary weekends. Not the tournament weekends. The ordinary ones. Let your athlete be sixteen sometimes. Let them be nine while they're nine.

The other children. Siblings are not support staff for one athlete's career. A childhood spent strapped into the back seat and parked in the bleachers of someone else's sport is a real cost, and it is invisible until one day it isn't — until the younger one says something at the dinner table that makes the whole family go quiet. Every child in the house deserves to be the main character of their own childhood, not a permanent extra in their sibling's.

The family's financial stability. When the spending creates genuine pressure in the house, that pressure does not stay in the house — it travels straight out to the field and lands on your athlete's shoulders. Athletes feel money stress even when you think you've hidden it, and "we spent so much

on this" becomes a weight they carry into every game. No youth sports investment is worth the family's security, and the math makes this almost absurd: only about one in ten parents even believes their child will reach the pros or the Olympics, and the real number who do is a tiny sliver of that. You are mortgaging certain things for an extraordinarily unlikely thing.

Faith, values, dinner, rest — whatever your family's non-negotiable rhythms are. Sports should fit inside your family's life. Your family's life should not be torn down and rebuilt to fit inside the sport. The Sunday dinner, the place of worship, the unhurried morning — those rhythms are the architecture of a childhood, and they are worth defending against a tournament schedule that would happily consume all of them.

The cost nobody itemizes

Picture an honest invoice for a single tournament weekend. The entry fee is on it. So is the hotel and the gas. But the real bill reads differently: two missed family dinners, one sibling's recital skipped, a Sunday of rest the body needed and didn't get, the homework done in a car, the marriage conversation that didn't happen because both parents were exhausted, the eight-year-old in the back seat who spent the weekend watching her brother instead of being an athlete herself. That's the true cost. And we pay it over and over, weekend after weekend, telling ourselves each one is just one weekend.

The hours add up the way water shapes a canyon — invisibly, and then permanently.

The line that keeps you honest

I'm not telling you to quit, pull back from everything, or refuse to chase excellence. Excellence is a beautiful thing to pursue, and sports can be one of the great gifts of a young life. I'm telling you to know what you're spending — all of it, not just the part on the invoice — and to decide on purpose rather than by drift.

Here is the line to remember, and it's the spine of this whole chapter: excellence is the goal; the family is the point. Pursue the first with everything you've got. Just never sacrifice the second to get it, because a family that wins the trophy and loses each other has won the wrong game entirely. The score you'll care about in twenty years isn't on any scoreboard. It's whether your athlete still wants to come home.

The Invoice Never Shows the Years

One of the hardest truths for parents is that the receipt only shows the money.

It does not show the years.

I can say this from the other side. My sons are grown now. I still get to watch them in different ways, and I am grateful for that, but I still see them as little boys. I still see a six-year-old sitting on the steps asking me to play catch and let him pitch. I still see the years when the game was simple, when the calendar did not yet own the family, when a backyard and a ball could hold a whole afternoon.

Those years do not come back.

This does not mean parents should avoid competition, travel, lessons, or serious development when those things fit. It means you should never surrender family time casually. Do not give away vacations, dinners, siblings' weekends, summer evenings, school events, quiet rides, and ordinary childhood moments just because someone else told you the window was closing.

The invoice shows the money.

It never shows the years.

Chapter Tool

The True Cost Audit

Before the next big youth-sports expense, add up what it actually costs — not just the invoice. Write down all of it: the registration, gear, travel, hotels, meals, and lessons; and then the things no invoice lists.

What will this cost in money this year? What will it cost in weekends and family time? What will it cost in my child's sleep, schoolwork, and rest? What will it cost the siblings? What will it cost the family's peace?

Then ask the only question that matters: Is what we get back worth what we are actually paying — across all of those lines, not just the one with a dollar sign? The invoice shows the money. It never shows the years. Make sure you are looking at both before you say yes.

Chapter 5: More Is Not Better

The Case for Ebb and Flow in Youth Sports

Somewhere along the way, youth sports adopted a religion, and it has only one commandment: more. More teams. More reps. More tournaments. More training. More travel. More exposure. More months of the year. The whole machine runs on a single unspoken belief — that development is a straight line, and the way you move your child faster along it is to pile on more of everything. If a little is good, a lot must be better, and the most must be best.

It's a seductive idea. It's also wrong — and not by a little. More is not better. Better is better. And most of the time, the road to better runs straight through less.

But before I make that case, I have to say the part that the "more" families never want to hear, the part that turns this from a training principle into a parenting one. Most of the time, the person adding the "more" isn't the child. It's us. The extra team, the second trainer, the year-round schedule — go back and ask honestly who wanted it first. More often than not, the answer is the parent, sitting in the fear that someone else's kid is getting ahead, buying "more" to quiet that fear for an afternoon. The child just carries what we sign them up for.

The lie inside the straight line

Here is what the religion of more refuses to admit: development is not linear, and you cannot force it to be by adding volume.

Athletes plateau. They regress. They go through stretches where they get worse before they leap — especially through puberty, when a growing body has to reorganize itself around new size and temporarily loses coordination it used to own. A child can work harder than ever and perform worse for two months, and that dip is often the runway for the biggest jump of their life.

When you don't understand that, "more" becomes your panic button. The plateau hits, so you add a trainer. The rough stretch comes, so you add a team. They look awkward, so you add reps. You are trying to override a natural rhythm by force, and all you actually accomplish is exhausting the one kid who needed time and rest to come out the other side. You can't fertilize your way past a season. You just burn the roots.

What ebb and flow actually looks like

I've watched it happen, and the two kids I think of most could not have ended up more differently.

I think of one twelve-year-old whose father reached out because, like so many good parents, he wanted an edge. At first, he thought the edge might be more baseball — another team, another place to be seen, another adult standing in front of his son. But once the family slowed down, the answer became much quieter. Travel ball was not really in the cards for them financially or time-wise, so they built a different kind of plan.

The boy started doing the work where most families overlook it: self-toss in the yard, wall ball when the weather turned, juggling to train his eyes and hands, small daily repetitions that did not need a hotel block or a tournament fee. His father told me later that the swings alone likely climbed into the tens of thousands over the years, not because an instructor demanded them, but because the athlete owned them. Alongside that came food, strength, school habits, laundry, cooking, and a household that became process-oriented instead of panic-oriented.

That is what "less" can do when it is chosen on purpose. Less travel did not mean less development. Less adult structure created more ownership. The athlete was not being under-served because he skipped some weekends. He was being protected from the idea that the only development worth trusting is the kind someone sells you.

That's the whole case, standing in two children. More didn't make the first one better. It used the first one up.

A healthy athletic year breathes. There is an in-season, when intensity is naturally high. A transition, when you wind down. A real off-season — genuine rest, a different sport, free play, a body that heals and a mind that gets to miss the game. Then a build back toward the next season. Push, recover, push, recover. The multi-sport athlete lives this rhythm automatically: the soccer player whose whole system gets a fresh stimulus when basketball starts, who comes back in spring hungry instead of fried.

This is why the research keeps landing in the same place: the multi-sport, well-rested kids stay healthier, fall in love more deeply, and go further in the long run than the early specializers who did "more" of one thing all year. The ebb is not time off from development. The ebb is development. Rest is not the absence of training. Rest is the part of training where the growth actually happens.

The courage to do less

Choosing less, in a culture that worships more, takes real nerve — because you will feel like you're falling behind in the exact moment another family adds the thing you skipped. You'll watch them sign up and feel the old fear close around your chest. Hold the line anyway. Give the off-week. Take the real off-season. Let them play the second sport, or no sport, for a season. Protect the Sunday.

And here is the cost, because there is always a cost and you deserve to know it before you choose: doing less may mean your child is, for a season, genuinely behind the kid who did more. The specializer might pull ahead at twelve. You have to be willing to be the family that looks less committed at the precise age when looking committed feels like everything. That's the price. Pay it anyway — because you will not be behind where it counts. You'll be the family whose athlete still has fresh legs in March, still loves the game in tenth grade, and is still playing, and still smiling, when half the "more" kids have quit the sport and resent the parent who couldn't stop adding to it.

More is not the plan. Better is the plan. And better has a rhythm. The only question is whether you have the nerve to honor it while the family next door is busy burning their kid's roots and calling it dedication.

Chapter Tool

The "More" Audit

Before adding any team, trainer, tournament, or training block, ask: Did my child ask for this, or did I? What am I actually afraid of if we don't do it? Is this adding development, or just adding activity? When, exactly, does my child rest this season — and if the honest answer is "they don't," that's not a schedule, it's a countdown to burnout. What would we have to give up — sleep, school, a second sport, family dinners, an off-season — to fit this in? And is what we gain worth what we'd lose?

If "more" can't survive those questions, it was never about development. It was about quieting fear — and there's a cheaper, kinder way to do that than spending your child's rest.

Part II — The Ten-Year Parent Roadmap

Chapter 6: Ages 6-9

Fun, Fundamentals, Movement, and Confidence

If you remember only one thing about the ages of six through nine, remember this: at this stage, the scoreboard is a liar, and joy is the only statistic that predicts the future.

I know that's hard to hear in a culture that's already ranking eight-year-olds. But I've watched youth sports from every angle for decades, and I can tell

you with complete confidence that almost nothing about who's "winning" at age eight tells you anything about who's playing at eighteen. What it tells you is who hit their growth early, whose parents started them young, or who happened to be the biggest athlete in a league sorted by birthday. None of that lasts. You know what lasts? Whether the athlete still wants to go.

So the entire job of this stage — for parents, for coaches, for everyone — is to make a child fall in love with moving their body and playing the game. That's it. That's the assignment. Everything else is downstream of it.

Why joy is the actual strategy

This isn't soft, feel-good advice. It's the hardest-nosed, most strategic thing I can tell you, and here's the math behind it: roughly seven out of ten athletes quit organized sports by age thirteen. Quit. Walk away. And they don't quit because they ran out of talent — they quit because somewhere along the line it stopped being fun. The single greatest predictor of whether your child is still playing (and therefore still developing) at fourteen, sixteen, eighteen is not their skill at eight. It's whether they still love it at eight.

Which means the parent obsessing over their second-grader's batting average, foot speed, or goal count is optimizing for the wrong thing entirely. They're polishing a statistic that doesn't matter while ignoring the only one that does. An athlete who can't stop smiling and can't wait for the next practice is winning at this age, even if they lose every game. A miserable, pressured, drilled-out eight-year-old who's technically advanced is losing, because they're heading straight for the exit, just a few years early.

What development actually looks like at 6-9

Forget specialization. Forget intensity. Forget the scoreboard. Here's what you actually want:

General athleticism over sport-specific skill. Running, jumping, climbing, throwing, catching, balancing, falling and getting up. Athletes who do lots of different movements — ideally across several sports and a ton of unstructured play — build a broad movement foundation that everything else gets layered onto later. The athlete who only does one sport at eight isn't ahead; they're narrow.

Fundamentals taught through play, not drills. At this age, learning should feel like a game, because a game is exactly how young children are built to learn. The best coaches at this level disguise the teaching inside fun. Cones become a dragon's lair. The skill gets learned because the athlete was too busy laughing to notice they were practicing.

Everyone plays, everyone touches it. A great 6-9 coach gives every athlete real reps and real playing time, full stop. A coach who's benching little athletes to win games or already cultivating "favorites" is a coach to walk away from, no matter how many medals are in the trophy case. At this age, equal opportunity isn't fairness for its own sake — it's development, because an athlete who stands and watches doesn't get better and doesn't fall in love.

Confidence built on effort, not outcome. Praise the try. Praise the hustle. Praise the getting-back-up. Confidence at this age is simply joy plus the belief that it's safe to try — and an athlete who feels that will attempt the hard thing, fail cheerfully, and try again. That willingness is worth more than any skill you could drill into them.

The parent's real job

Your job at this stage is almost embarrassingly simple, and most parents make it complicated because the culture told them to.

Keep it fun. Keep it light. Get them to lots of different kinds of movement. Protect their sleep, because at this age a regular bedtime does more for their development than any drill on earth. Feed them normal good food. And then — this is the hard part — get out of the way. Don't coach from the sideline. Don't review the game in the car. Don't compare your athlete to the big athlete who matured early. Don't sign up for the elite traveling team for seven-year-olds that some company invented to take your money.

When your child gets in the car after a game at this age, the only thing that should come out of your mouth is some version of "That looked fun — did you have fun?" Not "you should've passed more." Not "why didn't you hustle on that play." They are eight. The play does not matter. The love of the game matters, and you are either feeding it or starving it with every word.

The long view from the little fields

I've stood on the recruiting trail and evaluated athletes at the very top of the pyramid, and I've stood on a dewy Saturday field watching six-year-olds chase a ball in a giggling swarm. And I promise you the second scene is where the careers that last are actually being decided — not by who's best in the swarm, but by which of those athletes is having the most fun and will therefore still be playing a decade later when it finally starts to count.

So let the early bloomer's parents panic and push. Let them rank the eight-year-olds. You play a different game. You protect the joy, build the broad foundation, keep the bedtime, and let your athlete love it. You are not behind. You're playing the only version of this game that actually pays off. Work in silence, stack days, and let them have fun.

Chapter Tool

Ages 6-9 Parent Checklist

At this age, the goal is joy, movement, fundamentals, and confidence.

- [ ] My athlete still wants to go.

- [ ] Practices feel fun and age-appropriate.

- [ ] Everyone gets real reps and playing time.

- [ ] Adults are not treating the scoreboard like the point.

- [ ] My athlete is trying, laughing, failing, and coming back.

- [ ] We are not talking about rankings, elite teams, or future scholarships.

- [ ] Sleep, school, friends, and family life still matter.

Coach Beede Rule: Fun has to replace fear.

Chapter 7: Ages 10-12

Organic Repetition, Healthy Competition, and Local Growth

Ages ten through twelve are the quiet golden years of youth sports, and most families rush right through them looking for the next thing.

This is the stage where the joy you protected from six to nine starts turning into skill — where an athlete who loves the game begins, almost on their own, to get good at it. The fundamentals from those younger years now have somewhere to go. The body is coordinated enough to learn real technique, the attention span is long enough for actual teaching, and the love of the game is strong enough to power genuine repetition. It's a beautiful window. And the worst thing you can do is panic your way out of it by chasing

intensity, specialization, and exposure before the athlete is anywhere near needing any of it.

The magic word: organic

The kind of repetition that builds athletes at this age is organic — repetition driven by the athlete's own want, woven into play and a normal life, not force-fed through an adult-style grind.

Organic repetition is the athlete shooting in the driveway until dark because they feel like it. It's the backyard catch that goes on too long. It's the wall ball, the dribbling in the kitchen their mother pretends to hate, the thousand small reps an athlete racks up simply because they enjoy it. This is how skill is actually built at ten, eleven, twelve — not primarily through expensive private lessons, but through volume the athlete generates themselves because they love it.

Your job is to create the conditions for organic repetition and then let it happen. Put up the hoop. Get the net. Leave the ball where they'll trip over it. Take them to the open gym, the park, the field. And then resist the urge to turn every one of those moments into a coaching session, because the second the driveway becomes a lesson, the organic want dies and you're back to pushing.

Healthy competition — and the trap of the wrong kind

Competition becomes appropriate and valuable at this age. Athletes want to keep score now; they want to win, and learning to compete — to try hard, win with humility, lose without falling apart — is real development. So healthy competition is good.

But here's the trap: this is the age when families start mistaking the appearance of competition for the substance of development. They chase the "elite" team three towns over, the one with the trophies and the reputation, because winning at eleven feels like proof they're on the right track. And often what they've actually bought is a roster where their athlete rides the bench behind early-maturing athletes, gets fewer reps than they'd get on the local team, and learns that their value is conditional on the scoreboard.

A coach at this age who plays only the athletes who hit puberty first — who rides the big, early-developed athletes to win U12 tournaments while the late bloomers sit — is mortgaging your child's future for a banner. The athlete who's small at eleven might be your best athlete at sixteen, but not if these years taught them they don't belong on the field. Watch for whether playing

time tracks effort and growth or just size. That tells you whether you've found development or just a trophy operation.

Why local still wins

There's enormous, underrated value in growing up playing locally at this age — and the machine works hard to make you feel ashamed of it.

Local play means more actual playing time, less time wasted in cars and hotels, a body and schedule that aren't getting hammered by travel, money staying in your pocket, and an athlete who gets to also be an athlete — to have a neighborhood, friends outside the sport, a normal childhood with sports woven through it rather than bulldozing it. The relentless travel circuit at this age mostly serves the organizers, not the eleven-year-olds. As I've told families for years: the showcase-and-travel circuit is loud, expensive, and largely overrated for the average young athlete. What's underrated is a focused block of good local development where your athlete actually plays instead of sitting because the team is loaded with paying customers.

Quality over quantity. Always. An athlete getting hundreds of real reps in a good local environment is developing faster than an athlete getting a handful of at-bats from the bench of a glamorous travel team two states away.

Keep them multi-sport

Everything in the culture will push you toward specialization at this age. Resist it. The research is overwhelming and consistent: athletes who specialize early are roughly twice as likely to quit by fifteen and carry higher overuse-injury risk, while multi-sport athletes stay healthier, develop broader athleticism, fall in love more deeply, and go further. Let your eleven-year-old play two or three sports. The cross-training builds a better athlete, the variety protects the joy, and the different coaches and teammates build a more complete athlete. Specialization can come later, if and when the athlete chooses it. At ten, eleven, twelve, variety is the advantage.

The parent's evolving role

You're shifting from the joy-protector of the younger years toward becoming the quiet supporter of organic growth. Provide the equipment and the opportunities. Protect the sleep and the fuel, which still matter more than any drill. Keep them multi-sport. Choose development over trophies. And keep your mouth mostly shut on the technical stuff — they have coaches for that, and your relationship is too valuable to spend on driveway corrections.

These are the years skill quietly compounds. Don't rush them, don't over-program them, don't chase the shiny thing. Put up the hoop, get out of the way, choose the environment where your athlete actually plays and grows, and let the love of the game do the heavy lifting. Let the skill build itself.

The Mechanics Trap

There is a danger in youth sports that sounds responsible at first: teaching perfect mechanics too early.

In baseball, it may be the perfect swing. In softball, the perfect throwing motion. In basketball, the perfect shooting form. In soccer, the perfect touch. In lacrosse, the perfect release. In hockey, the perfect stride. In volleyball, the perfect arm swing. In tennis, the perfect stroke.

Mechanics matter. Fundamentals matter. Good instruction matters.

But at ages ten through twelve, the athlete is still learning how to move, feel, adjust, fail, compete, and self-organize. When adults overload that athlete with technical language before the body and mind are ready, the athlete can become stiff, robotic, confused, and afraid to move freely.

A voice can be knowledgeable and still be wrong for your athlete's age, body, confidence, and stage.

At young ages, the goal is not perfect mechanics. The goal is usable movement, growing confidence, and the ability to adjust.

Feel comes before polish.

Freedom comes before perfection.

Development comes before correction.

A young athlete cannot compete freely if every movement feels wrong.

Repetition Leads to Retention

The foundation of skill is repetition, but not every repetition has to be purchased in 30- or 60-minute blocks.

Playing catch counts. Wall ball counts. Wiffle ball counts. Backyard games count. Pickup games count. Shooting in the driveway counts. Kicking a ball against a wall counts. Throwing a football, playing dodgeball, juggling,

skating, swimming, climbing, sprinting, jumping, and learning how the body moves all count.

Parents often chase structured repetitions because structured repetitions look more serious. But unstructured repetitions are where athletes build feel. They learn rhythm, timing, creativity, problem-solving, and confidence.

Before paying for more instruction, ask whether your athlete has accumulated enough simple, healthy, age-appropriate repetitions.

Do not coach the athlete out of the child.

Chapter Tool

Ages 10-12 Development Check

Ask these questions before adding more structure.

1. Is my athlete still enjoying the sport?

2. Are they getting real repetitions, or just wearing a better uniform?

3. Is the coach teaching in simple, progression-based language?

4. Is the environment rewarding effort and growth, not just early size?

5. Are we still protecting multi-sport play, rest, and local community?

6. Are we adding a lesson because the athlete wants it, or because I am afraid?

7. Is this helping development, or just making us busier?

Parent reset: Repetition leads to retention, but not every repetition needs to be scripted by an adult.

Chapter 8: Ages 13-14

The Comparison Window

Ages thirteen and fourteen may be the single most dangerous window in all of youth sports — not because of anything the athletes do, but because of what the adults around them start believing.

This is the stage where bodies stop developing on the same schedule. Some athletes grow early and suddenly look like young adults — taller, stronger, faster, more physical. Others are late bloomers who feel like they shrank overnight relative to their peers: smaller, slower, behind. Social pressure

spikes. Rankings appear. Adults start talking more seriously, in lower voices, about who "has it." Social media makes every one of these differences public and permanent-feeling. And right here, in this window, is where I've watched more parents lose perspective — and make more damaging permanent decisions — than at any other age.

The mirage that fools everyone

Here's what happens. A parent watches an early-maturing athlete run faster, jump higher, throw harder, hit farther, skate stronger, dominate physically. And the parent's gut whispers the most dangerous lie in youth sports: the race is being decided right now, and my athlete is on the wrong side of it.

It is not being decided. It is not close to being decided. What that parent is actually watching is not talent — it's puberty, arriving on different athletes at different times. The "stud" at thirteen is frequently just the athlete who matured first, winning on physical maturity that everyone else will eventually get too. And the late bloomer who looks "behind" is often the athlete who's quietly building skill, feel, and competitive toughness because they've had to win without the size — and who becomes lethal the moment their body finally catches up.

I have seen this story play out hundreds of times, and the ending is almost always the opposite of what the thirteen-year-old scoreboard predicted. The dominant early athlete who never had to develop real skill gets passed and quits, baffled, at sixteen. The "small" athlete who learned to score over bigger defenders grows five inches and is suddenly unguardable. Development is not a staircase you can rank people on. It's a roller coaster — athletes plateau, regress, get awkward, lose coordination, lose and regain confidence, stumble, and then make leaps no ranking could have predicted.

So burn this into your mind as a parent of a thirteen- or fourteen-year-old: a suddenly awkward athlete is not broken. A late-developing athlete is not finished. An early star is not guaranteed. And a ranking at thirteen is not a verdict — it's a weather report on a single day.

The cardinal rule of this window

Because development is a temporary, chaotic, uneven process at this age, the cardinal rule is simple and absolute: do not make permanent decisions during a temporary stage of development.

Don't quit the sport because your athlete suddenly looks slow next to the boy who grew early — that's temporary. Don't write off your child's future because a ranking didn't include them at thirteen — that's a snapshot. Don't pour the family's money into emergency fixes because of a six-month dip that's actually just a growth spurt scrambling coordination. And on the other side: don't let an early bloomer (or their parents) get crowned and coast, because the field is coming. The permanent decision made in a temporary moment is the great tragedy of this age window, and almost all of them are made out of fear of a mirage.

What actually starts to matter here

This is also the stage where the real developmental habits start to matter in a serious way — not adult-style overload, but genuine building blocks:

Nutrition becomes important, because the body is growing fast and needs fuel — and the danger here flips from "too much junk" to under-fueling, not eating enough to cover growth plus activity. Sleep is at a premium and chronically shorted; it's when growth and recovery literally happen. Recovery becomes a real thing to respect. Safe, supervised strength training can begin — with light loads, perfect technique, and a qualified coach, built around the athlete's training age, not their birthday. Sprint mechanics, mobility, body awareness. And the beginnings of self-ownership — the athlete starting to take responsibility for their own development.

A journal can help here — a simple weekly check-in (what went well, what to work on, what I enjoyed, how my energy felt). A qualified strength coach can help. But a calm parent who refuses to panic at the mirage can help most of all. The growth-spurt years are turbulent enough inside the athlete's own body; the last thing they need is a frightened adult adding turbulence from the outside.

The parent's job shifts

Your role begins a real shift in this window. The athlete needs to start understanding two things at once — who they are today (an in-progress, changing, sometimes-awkward work) and who they're trying to become. You're no longer the joy-protector of the early years or just the supporter of organic reps. You're becoming the steady hand on a roller coaster, the calm voice that says this is normal, you're not behind, your body is doing exactly what it's supposed to, keep working and trust the process.

So here is the whole chapter in three lines, the three things a parent of a thirteen-year-old must hold onto when the comparison window starts screaming:

Do not let the early bloomer create panic. Do not let the late bloomer lose hope. And do not let a temporary stage make a permanent decision.

Work in silence. Stack days. Let the athlete become.

The Reclassification Question: Are We Buying Development Time or Anxiety Time?

One of the clearest signs that youth sports has changed is that parents are no longer only being asked to spend money.
They are being asked to manipulate time.

Repeating 8th grade. Reclassifying. Delaying graduation. Taking a gap year. Choosing an academy. Trying to buy physical maturity, recruiting visibility, or a perceived age advantage.

There are situations where an extra year can make sense. A young person may need more academic readiness, more emotional maturity, more time after an injury, or a better school environment. Some families make that decision thoughtfully for reasons that serve the whole child.

That is not what concerns me.

What concerns me is when a family begins altering a child's academic and social timeline because the youth sports environment has convinced them their athlete is falling behind.

That is the redshirt trap.

It usually shows up in the comparison window. Ages thirteen and fourteen. One athlete matures early. Another is still waiting on puberty. One athlete is taller, stronger, faster, more physical. Another looks temporarily behind. Parents see the difference and panic.

Then someone says the quiet part out loud: maybe we should repeat 8th grade.

Before a parent makes that decision, they need to step back.

Are we doing this because our athlete truly needs more time academically, emotionally, socially, or physically?

Or are we doing this because another athlete grew first?

Those are very different reasons.

A redshirt year may buy time. But parents must ask what kind of time they are buying.

Development time?

Academic time?

Emotional time?

Or anxiety time?

Do not make a permanent academic and social decision because of a temporary physical-development window.

Your athlete's body is on its own clock. Their confidence is still forming. Their friendships matter. Their school experience matters. Their identity matters. Their childhood matters.

An extra year may be right for some families. But it should never be purchased with panic.

The better question

is not, "Will this give my athlete an advantage?"

The better question

is, "Does this serve the whole person we are raising?"
That is the 40-year question.

Post-Grad Is Not One Thing

Parents also need to understand that post-grad, reclassification, and extra-development years are not all the same thing.

There is a major difference between an athletic-centric academy selling more training time and a legitimate academic institution offering structure, maturity, rigor, community, relationships, and a better runway into college. One may be built primarily around sport. The other may be built around the whole young person.

That difference matters.

A post-grad year or reclass year at a real academic institution should be a 40-year decision, not a four-year panic move. It should serve the student, the athlete, the family, and the person your athlete is becoming. It should not be chosen because social media made parents afraid, because another athlete

grew first, because a showcase operator implied the door was closing, or because an adult told you the only way to compete later is to manipulate time now.

Reclassifying and post-grad are not for the masses. They are for a specific athlete and family seeking balance, preparation, maturity, and a plan.

If the reason is academic readiness, emotional maturity, school fit, health, recovery, or a truly thoughtful developmental path, the conversation can be worthwhile.

If the reason is mostly panic, pause.

The extra year should make the whole person better, not just make the parent feel temporarily safer.

Chapter Tool

Season Start Family Meeting

Before each season, sit together and answer:
1. Why are we playing this season?

2. What does the athlete want from this season?

3. What does the family want to protect?

4. What are our non-negotiables?

5. What is our budget?

6. What is our time limit?

7. What does success look like besides winning?

8. What will we do if the athlete loses joy?

9. What will we do if school begins to slip?

10. What sentence will we repeat when fear shows up?

Suggested sentence: We will not let fear make the plan.

Chapter 9: Ages 15-17

Ownership, Accountability, and Raising the Floor
By fifteen, the game changes.

Not because the dream suddenly becomes real. Not because recruiting is now some magical clock that starts ticking over every athlete's head. Not because a freshman, sophomore, or junior performance determines the rest of a young person's life.

The game changes because the athlete must begin changing.

A fifteen-year-old is no longer a little child being carried through youth sports by a parent's schedule, a coach's instructions, and a weekend calendar. They are stepping into high school, into heavier academic demands, into more complex social environments, into bodies that are still changing, into more competitive teams, into conversations about future fit, and into a stage of life where ownership becomes non-negotiable.

This is the age where parents have to begin asking a hard question:

Does the dream belong to the athlete yet?

Because if the dream still belongs mostly to the parent, the next few years will expose it.

The handoff becomes real

At ages six through nine, parents protect joy.

At ages ten through twelve, parents protect organic growth and healthy competition.

At ages thirteen and fourteen, parents protect patience through the comparison window.

At ages fifteen through seventeen, parents must begin protecting ownership.

That means the athlete starts carrying more of the process.

They need to begin owning their communication with coaches. They need to begin owning their routines. They need to understand nutrition, sleep, strength, school, recovery, body language, effort, and preparation. They need to know how to ask for feedback. They need to know how to handle a role they do not love. They need to know how to respond when they are not selected, not starting, not ranked, not noticed, not yet where they want to be.

That is not punishment. That is preparation.

If a parent keeps carrying every part of the journey at this age, the athlete loses the opportunity to become the kind of young person coaches want and life requires.

College coaches notice ownership. High school coaches notice it. Teachers notice it. Employers will notice it later.

A young person who can speak for themselves, prepare themselves, recover from difficulty, and take responsibility for their own improvement is becoming more than an athlete.

They are becoming an adult.

Raise the floor

Most parents are obsessed with ceiling.
How good can they become?

How high can they go?

What is the best possible school, team, ranking, level, or outcome?

There is nothing wrong with dreaming. Dreams matter. They pull young people forward. But the daily work is not really about the ceiling. The daily work is about the floor.

The ceiling is the best version of the athlete on their best day.

The floor is who they are when things are not going well.

Can they still compete when they are tired?
Can they still be a good teammate when they are not playing?

Can they still handle school when the schedule gets heavy?

Can they still take coaching when their confidence is shaken?

Can they still eat, sleep, recover, and prepare when nobody is watching?

Can they still control body language after a mistake?

Can they still show up the next day?

That is the floor.

Coaches trust the floor. Programs trust the floor. Life rewards the floor.

A young athlete with a high ceiling and a low floor is a roller coaster. Brilliant one day, unreliable the next. A young athlete with a steadily rising floor becomes trustworthy. Their worst day gets better. Their habits become stronger. Their response to adversity becomes steadier.

Raise the floor, and the ceiling will rise.

That line should become part of your family's language.

What ownership looks like

Ownership at fifteen through seventeen does not mean the athlete has everything figured out. They will still need guidance. They will still make mistakes. They will still forget things, misread situations, respond emotionally, and need help.

Ownership means they are beginning to carry the right things.

They own their schoolwork. Not perfectly, but honestly. They know when assignments are due. They ask for help. They understand that academics are not separate from athletics. Grades reveal habits: time management, discipline, accountability, maturity.

They own their body. They understand that sleep is not optional, food is fuel, strength must be built responsibly, recovery is part of training, and playing exhausted or under-fueled is not toughness.

They own their communication. If they want more opportunity, they learn to ask a coach, "What do I need to improve to earn more time?" If they do not understand their role, they ask, "What do you need from me right now?" Parents can rehearse these conversations at home, but the athlete must increasingly have them.

They own their attitude. They stop blaming every coach, official, teammate, condition, or circumstance. They learn the difference between an excuse and an explanation. They understand that body language is always being read.

They own their dream. That is the biggest one. A parent can support the dream. A parent can help resource the dream. A parent can drive, pay, encourage, guide, and advocate when appropriate. But by fifteen, sixteen, seventeen, the dream has to be moving into the athlete's hands.

If the parent wants it more than the athlete does, the athlete will eventually feel trapped inside someone else's ambition.

What parents still do

Stepping back does not mean disappearing.

This is where parents often misunderstand the handoff. They think they have two choices: control everything or abandon the athlete to figure it out alone. Neither is right.

At this stage, the parent becomes a guide.

You help them think. You help them evaluate fit. You help them slow down when emotion is high. You help them understand the cost of decisions. You help them find credible resources. You help them protect their health. You help them remember they are more than the sport.

But you do not write every email.

You do not fight every playing-time battle.

You do not run the whole schedule without their input.

You do not make the dream yours and ask them to perform it.

The parent becomes the person behind the athlete, not the person in front of them.

That is a powerful difference.

The recruiting illusion

Ages fifteen through seventeen are also when the recruiting conversation starts to get louder, and this is where many parents lose balance.

They begin thinking every performance is being judged. Every event could matter. Every coach might be watching. Every mistake feels expensive.

But the truth is much calmer than the fear.

Most athletes are not ready to be meaningfully evaluated until their body, maturity, skill set, academic profile, and personal desire begin lining up. That timeline varies by sport, gender, level, and individual development, but one principle holds: visibility before readiness does not help.

A young athlete should not chase exposure before they have built something worth exposing.

At this age, the better focus is not panic. It is preparation.

Build the body.

Build the transcript.

Build the habits.

Build the character.

Build the skill.

Build the communication.

Build the floor.

Then, when the right people are watching at the right time, there is something real to see.

The parent's hardest truth

Sometimes, around this age, a parent realizes the athlete does not want the dream as much as the parent does.

That is painful.

But it is also necessary information.

A young person may love the sport and not want the college grind. They may enjoy being on a varsity team and not want to build their life around recruiting. They may have other interests, other gifts, other versions of themselves beginning to emerge.

That is not failure.

Sports did not fail because the athlete stops at high school. Sports did its job if the athlete learned how to compete, prepare, handle disappointment, work with others, take care of their body, and become a more resilient young person.

The long game is not college athletics.

The long game is the human being.

So at fifteen through seventeen, help your athlete dream. Help them work. Help them own the process. Help them raise the floor. But also help them tell the truth about what they want.

The dream must belong to them.

If it does, support it with wisdom.
If it does not, love them enough to let the dream change.

Talented Is Not the Same as Recruitable

By the high school years, parents often ask the wrong question.
They ask, "Is my athlete talented?"

Coaches are asking something deeper: "Is this athlete recruitable?"

Those are not the same question.

Talent gets a coach's attention. Recruitability earns a coach's trust.

A recruitable athlete is not simply the athlete with the best stats, strongest arm, fastest time, biggest body, or flashiest highlight reel. A recruitable athlete has traits that translate into the next environment.

Can the athlete play at the level? That includes skill, physical tools, speed, strength, decision-making, sport IQ, and projectability.

Can the athlete handle the environment? That includes academics, maturity, time management, independence, communication, nutrition, sleep, recovery, and daily habits.

Can the athlete be trusted in the program? That includes coachability, body language, character, teammate behavior, response to failure, and ownership.

A coach is not only recruiting the performance. A coach is recruiting the person who has to live inside the program every day.

Compete. Execute. Handle the Workload.

Before worrying about recruiting, ask three harder questions.
Can my athlete compete?

Can my athlete execute?

Can my athlete handle the workload mentally and physically?

Those questions cut through hype. They also return the family to preparation. The athlete who cannot yet execute basic skills under pressure does not need more exposure. The athlete who cannot handle disappointment does not need a bigger stage. The athlete who cannot recover, sleep, eat, train, communicate, study, and respond to coaching does not need a new logo.

They need preparation.

Prepared is different than promoted.

Rankings promote. Highlights promote. Social media promotes. Some events promote. But the next level exposes preparation. It asks whether the athlete can compete against better athletes, execute when the game speeds up, and manage the workload that comes with being in a serious environment.

Do not worry about recruiting until your athlete is recruitable.

Chapter Tool

Athlete Ownership Journal

Use once a week. 1. One thing I did well this week:
2. One thing I need to improve:

3. One thing I enjoyed:

4. Energy, mood, and body check: Energy: _____ / 10 Mood: _____ / 10 Body: _____ / 10 5. One habit I controlled this week:

6. One thing I will own next week:

Chapter 10: The Athlete Handoff

When Parents Step Back and Athletes Step Forward

Everything you've done as a sports parent — every drive, every fee, every early morning, every word in the car — has been building toward a single moment most parents never consciously plan for: the handoff.

The handoff is the gradual, deliberate transfer of ownership of the athletic journey from your hands into your child's. And here's the truth that should reframe how you see your whole job: the entire point of being a great sports parent is to make yourself progressively unnecessary. If you're still running the whole show when your athlete is seventeen, you didn't succeed at sports parenting — you skipped its most important lesson. The goal was never to manage an athlete. It was to raise one who can manage themselves.

Why the handoff is the whole game

Think about what you're actually trying to produce. Not a trophy. Not a scholarship. A capable young adult who can set a goal, do the work, handle a setback, talk to an authority figure, advocate for themselves, and own their choices. The sport is just the training ground where those capacities get built — and they only get built if, at some point, you hand the athlete the controls.

A young athlete who owns their own journey practices and works because they want to, not because you nagged. They talk to their own coach. They manage their own gear and schedule. They decide how hard to chase the dream — because it's actually their dream by then. That athlete develops drive, resilience, and self-direction that will serve them for forty years, in every arena of life. The athlete who never gets handed the controls stays dependent, fragile, and — this is the part parents miss — often quietly resentful, because deep down they know they're living someone else's plan.

I've sat across the desk from both kinds as a college coach, and I could tell them apart in the first five minutes. One athlete answers my questions. The other looks at Mom and Dad before answering. One athlete emailed me himself. The other had every message written by a parent. College coaches notice this instantly, and it shapes who they recruit, because they're not looking for a player they have to parent — they're looking for a young adult

who can handle the next level. The handoff isn't just good parenting. It's the thing that makes your athlete recruitable.

It's a dimmer, not a switch

The handoff is not a single dramatic moment where you suddenly step away. It's a gradual dial you turn over the better part of a decade, matching the athlete's growing capacity.

At six, you handle essentially everything — all the logistics, all the communication, all the decisions. That's appropriate; they're six. But every year after that, you hand over a little more. By ten or eleven, the athlete can pack their own bag and start taking responsibility for being ready. By the early teens, they can begin talking to their own coach about small things and driving their own organic practice. By the mid-teens, the athlete should be having their own conversations about their role and their playing time, managing their own training, and owning the dream. By the time they're heading toward the next level, you should be a consultant they choose to call — not the manager running their career.

Each year, you do a little less for them and a little more with them, until you're mostly just watching them do it themselves. Turn the dial too slowly and you produce a dependent seventeen-year-old who can't function without you. Turn it too fast and you abandon an athlete who wasn't ready. Read your actual child and turn it at the speed they can handle — but always, always keep turning it in the same direction: toward them.

The hard part is yours, not theirs

Let me be honest about who struggles most with the handoff. It's not the athletes. It's us.

Stepping back is genuinely hard for a parent who's invested years, money, love, and identity into a child's sport. It can feel like losing relevance, like being benched yourself, like watching them make decisions you'd make differently. There's a real grief in it. And there's fear — what if they don't work as hard without me pushing? What if they make the wrong call? What if they decide they don't want it as much as I do?

Those fears are exactly why the handoff matters. Because if the drive only exists when you're pushing, it was never their drive — it was yours, borrowed. If they can't make a decision without you, they're not ready for a world that will demand thousands of decisions you won't be there for. And if, when you finally hand them the dream, they decide they don't want to

chase it as hard as you would have — that is painful, but it is information you needed, and far better learned at fifteen than discovered at twenty-five in a life they never chose. As I've said about the seats I've sat in, the hardest one by far is the parent's. The handoff is where that's most true.

Handing it over without dropping it

Stepping back doesn't mean disappearing. You don't stop being their parent, their biggest fan, their safe place to land, the person who says "I love watching you play" no matter the result. You stop being their manager. There's a world of difference, and your athlete feels it instantly: the parent in the stands who's enjoying them versus the one running their career from the third row.

So hand it over on purpose, a little each year, with your eyes open. Let them carry more. Let them talk to the coach. Let them own the work and the dream. Be there to catch them, advise them when they ask, and love them regardless — but let them drive. That's not stepping away from your job. That's your job finally being done well.

The best thing you will ever do for your athlete is make yourself unnecessary — and then watch, from the stands, as they prove you succeeded.

Chapter Tool

Puberty and Comparison Parent Reset

When comparison starts taking over, ask:
- Am I comparing my athlete to an early bloomer?

- Am I mistaking puberty for permanent ability?

- Am I reacting to a ranking, team list, or social media post?

- Is my athlete in a temporary awkward growth phase?

- Are we protecting nutrition, sleep, recovery, and confidence?

- Are we making a permanent decision during a temporary stage?

Say to your athlete: You are not behind. You are becoming. Your body is on its own clock. Keep working.

Special Section: Ages 10-16 — Prepare, Don't

Panic Parents of athletes between ten and sixteen often feel as if every year is a deadline.

It is not.

Ages ten through sixteen are not a single recruiting runway. They are a development arc.

Ages 10-12: Build the Athlete The priorities are joy, repetition, fundamentals, coordination, movement, and confidence. The athlete should be learning through play and simple competition. They should play catch, shoot, kick, throw, skate, run, jump, climb, compete, and explore. They should try things, fall, fail, and return.

The parent question is not, "Are we doing enough?"

The better question

is, "Is my athlete building a foundation and still loving it?"

Ages 12-14: Grow Through the Middle The priorities are growth, maturity, learning style, healthy challenge, program fit, and patience. This is where athletes begin to see difference. Some grow early. Some grow late. Some look advanced because puberty arrived first. Others are quietly building skill.

Parents should not panic here.

They should watch the whole athlete: confidence, sleep, nutrition, recovery, school, friendships, coachability, and desire.

Ages 14-16: Prepare for Competition The priorities become preparation, strength, sport IQ, execution, accountability, and workload management. This is when athletes begin learning what high school and future competitive environments will require.

Can they compete?

Can they execute?

Can they handle the workload mentally and physically?

Those questions matter more than rankings, early recruiting noise, or social media attention.

The Parent Reset You cannot control the competition.

You can only help prepare the athlete.

Take control of childhood. Build the foundation. Protect the joy. Prepare without panic.

Part III — The Inner Athlete

Chapter 11: Mental Toughness Rewritten

What Toughness Really Means — and What It Does Not

We need to rescue the phrase mental toughness, because somewhere along the way adults took a useful idea and turned it into a costume. They made toughness mean silence through pain. No emotion. No doubt. No fear. No tears. No need for help. They made it sound like a child who struggles should simply harden up, push through, and stop feeling whatever they're feeling.

That is not toughness. That is emotional numbness wearing toughness as a disguise — and before we go further, I want to name where most kids learn to put that costume on. They learn it from us. They learn it the first time a parent's face tightens at a tear, the first time "you're okay, shake it off" arrives a half-second too fast, the first time they sense that the emotion they're feeling is unwelcome in the car. Children are students of their parents' faces. Long before a coach ever tells a kid to toughen up, most have already read it in the people they love most.

Real mental toughness is not the absence of fear, frustration, nerves, doubt, or pain. Every athlete who cares feels those things. The question was never whether the athlete feels them. The question is what the athlete does next.

Mental toughness is the ability to take the next right action when it's uncomfortable, when you're afraid, and when you don't feel like it. That's it. It isn't dramatic or loud. It's often quiet, unglamorous, and invisible from the stands. It's the kid who makes the mistake and gets back in position. Who gets corrected and listens instead of crumbling. Who is nervous and competes anyway. Who loses and comes back to work. Who can say "I'm not okay" instead of performing fine. Feel it, then function. That is the whole of it.

Why pressure alone doesn't build it

Here's where good, loving parents get it backwards. They believe toughness is built by adding pressure — criticize harder, demand more, remove comfort, make the child prove they can take it. And there's a sliver of truth in it: kids do need challenge, standards, and accountability; the world will not rearrange itself around their comfort.

But pressure without safety doesn't build toughness. It builds fear. A child who believes that love, approval, or belonging depends on performance does not get tougher. They get anxious. They get perfectionistic. They get very good at hiding. They may even perform for a while — and the whole time, underneath, the sport is quietly becoming a place of danger instead of a place of joy.

The strongest athletes I've ever been around were the ones who knew, all the way down, that they were loved before the game started and loved after it ended. That security didn't make them soft. It did the opposite. It gave them permission to take risks, room to fail, and freedom to compete without feeling that one mistake would change who they were in their parent's eyes. Toughness grows in safety, not in fear. A child with a secure base can go be brave. A child without one is just managing their anxiety in cleats.

What the misread actually costs

I had to learn to recognize the real thing, because for a long time I was looking for the wrong version of it.

This is not a story about ignoring injury or pushing through pain that needed medical attention. If a young athlete is hurt, the body comes first. The point is not that Mary played injured. The point is that she felt fear, pressure, and doubt — and once it was safe for her to compete, she stepped forward anyway.

I think of a girl named Mary. She was eleven or twelve, playing in our youth soccer program, and she came from a family of athletes — an older brother who played hockey, a dad who pushed hard. Mary herself was tough in the ways people usually mean it; she'd played hockey on an all-boys team. But toughness isn't only the loud kind, and the moment I remember most about her had nothing to do with how hard she could hit.

She'd picked up an injury, and she was scared — scared it would keep her from playing the way she expected of herself, and, more than that, scared of disappointing her dad and her brother. You could see it on her. Her brother had called her soft. The message from the men who loved her was the old one: you're not bleeding, nothing's broken, go play. And here is the part that mattered, the part that had nothing to do with the scoreboard: she was hurting and afraid, and she made the quiet decision to go out and compete anyway — not to prove them wrong, but because her team needed her and she'd decided that mattered more than her fear.

That was the toughness. Right there. Not gritted teeth, not silence, not pretending she wasn't scared — she was plainly scared. She felt it, and then she functioned. As it happened, she went on to score the tying goal and then the game-winner on a penalty kick, and that's a wonderful ending. But I want to be careful, because the goals are not why the story belongs here. She'd have shown the exact same toughness if that penalty kick had sailed over the bar. The courage was the decision to step onto the field afraid. The goals were just a bonus the courage happened to earn.

That's the toughness worth building — and notice it had nothing to do with not feeling the hard thing. It was about what came after the feeling.

Parents confuse toughness with intensity. They see a child upset after a mistake and think, "they need to toughen up." Sometimes that's even true — sometimes a kid does need to learn to reset and compete through frustration. But sometimes the child isn't soft at all. Sometimes they're overloaded. Under-rested. Carrying expectations too heavy for their age. Afraid to fail because every mistake gets reviewed in the car. Convinced their parent's face changes with the scoreboard.

If that last one landed, sit with it for a second, because it's the one most of us are guiltiest of and least aware of. A child who has learned to watch your face for the verdict isn't building toughness. They're building a habit of performing for approval that can follow them into every relationship they'll ever have. So if you want a mentally tough athlete, don't start with the child. Start with the environment. Start with the language at home, the temperature of the car ride, and whether your kid can tell you a hard truth without it costing them your warmth.

The tools, and what parents can say

A mentally tough athlete gradually learns four things, and a parent can nurture all four without ever once saying "toughen up." They learn to reset — one mistake doesn't get to own the next moment. They learn to receive coaching — to take correction without collapsing or arguing, a skill that will outlast sports by fifty years. They learn to compete when conditions aren't perfect — bad weather, bad calls, poor sleep, a tough draw. And they learn to tell the truth — to say "I'm nervous," "I'm tired," "I need help," and keep going anyway. Honesty is not the opposite of toughness. Honesty is part of it.

After a hard moment, most parents say too much — they lecture, diagnose, compare, and turn one bad game into a seminar on effort and the future. The child rarely needs that. They need a calm place to land. "I love watching you play." "You don't have to talk about it yet." "When you're ready, we'll figure out what you learned." "What's the next right action?" Those sentences separate the child from the performance. They acknowledge the hard thing without panic. And they point toward action without shame.

That is how toughness is actually built — not by teaching a child that hard things are easy, but by standing beside them, steady and unafraid, while the hard thing stays hard. Be the secure base. The bravery grows from there.

Chapter Tool

Mental Toughness Parent Language Guide

Use these: "What's the next right action?" · "You can feel disappointed and still respond well." · "One mistake doesn't own the next play." · "Tell the truth, then do the work." · "Being nervous doesn't mean you're not ready." · "Tough doesn't mean silent. Tough means accountable." · "Failure is information, not identity."

Retire these: "Stop being soft." · "You didn't want it enough." · "Real athletes don't get nervous." · "Do you know how much this costs?" · "You embarrassed yourself." · "You have to be tougher than that."

The first list builds a child who can come back from anything. The second builds one who learns to hide from you. You're choosing one or the other every time you open your mouth after a hard game.

Chapter 12: Confidence at Every Age

Joy at 8, Willingness at 12, Resilience at 14, Identity at 17
Confidence does not look the same at every age.

That is one of the biggest mistakes parents make. They expect confidence to sound like certainty, swagger, dominance, or visible belief. They want the eight-year-old to act like the seventeen-year-old. They want the twelve-year-old to be unbothered by failure. They want the fourteen-year-old to look steady while their body is changing every month.

But confidence develops in stages, just like the athlete does.

If parents understand the stage, they can protect the right thing.

If they misunderstand the stage, they can damage confidence while trying to build it.

Confidence at eight is joy

At eight, confidence looks like "watch this."

It looks like a young athlete who wants to run back onto the field, court, rink, mat, pool deck, or track. It looks like laughing after a mistake. It looks like trying something without fear that a parent will correct every movement. It looks like wanting to go again.

Do not overcomplicate confidence at this age.

If the athlete still lights up, confidence is alive.

The greatest mistake at this stage is turning performance into the measure. Parents watch for talent. The better question is whether the athlete feels safe trying.

An eight-year-old who feels safe trying will develop.

An eight-year-old who plays scared will eventually protect themselves by pulling away.

Confidence at twelve is willingness

At twelve, confidence becomes the willingness to try the harder thing.

This is the age where athletes begin to notice differences. Who is bigger? Who is faster? Who gets picked first? Who made the better team? Who is getting extra training? Who is talked about by adults?

Comparison begins to enter the room.

So confidence at twelve is not always loud. Sometimes it is simply the willingness to keep stepping into challenge.

Will they try the new position? Will they face the stronger opponent? Will they keep practicing something they are not yet good at? Will they risk looking awkward? Will they compete without needing every outcome to feel safe?

That is confidence.

The parent's job at this stage is not to remove difficulty. It is to make sure difficulty does not become humiliation.

A young athlete who can be challenged and still feel supported is in the right environment.

Confidence at fourteen is resilience

At fourteen, confidence is tested by the comparison window.

Bodies change. Some athletes mature early. Some look temporarily behind. Social pressure rises. Rankings appear. Playing time changes. Coaches begin making harder decisions. Athletes may suddenly feel awkward in bodies that used to feel familiar.

Confidence at this age is not believing everything will go well.

Confidence is being able to say:

"I played badly, but I am not bad."

"I am behind physically right now, but I am not finished."

"I made a mistake, but I can still compete."

"I do not like my role, but I can still work."

This is where parents must be careful.

A fourteen-year-old can look strong and still be fragile inside. A young athlete at this age may be deeply affected by a parent's face, a coach's comment, a social media post, a ranking, or one comparison to a teammate.

The parent's job is to anchor confidence to something deeper than the scoreboard and the body.

Effort. Character. Growth. Work. Integrity. Response.

Those are the anchors.

Confidence at seventeen is identity

By seventeen, true confidence is not swagger.
True confidence is identity that does not collapse when performance does.

A confident seventeen-year-old knows they are an athlete, but not only an athlete. They can have a hard game and still be whole. They can be corrected and still be steady. They can dream about the next level without believing their entire worth depends on it.

That kind of confidence is rare.

It is built over years by adults who kept love separate from performance.

A seventeen-year-old whose identity is entirely tied to sport is vulnerable. An injury can crush them. A coach's decision can define them. A lost role can make them feel like they lost themselves.

A whole athlete can still be disappointed. They can still hurt. They can still grieve. But they do not disappear when the sport does not go their way.

That is the kind of confidence parents should be building from the beginning.

What destroys confidence fastest

The fastest way to destroy confidence is conditional approval.

A parent whose warmth rises and falls with performance may never say love is conditional. But athletes read the room. They read the face in the stands, the tone in the car, the silence after a mistake, the energy at dinner.

They know.

If the great game earns joy and the bad game earns distance, the athlete learns the rule quickly.

Perform well, and home feels safe.

Perform badly, and home gets cold.

That is devastating.

The athlete may still perform. They may even perform well. But they are not building healthy confidence. They are building a nervous dependence on approval.

Confidence grows when the athlete knows the relationship is safe before, during, and after competition.

A parent's steady love is not a small thing.

It may be the most important performance environment the athlete ever has.

What builds confidence

Confidence is built when athletes are allowed to try, fail, learn, and return without shame.

It is built when effort is noticed. It is built when coaches teach instead of humiliate. It is built when parents ask better questions. It is built when the athlete owns part of the process. It is built when comparison is named and rejected. It is built when athletes have a life outside the sport. It is built when home remains home.

Confidence is not something parents can simply give with praise. Praise helps, but empty praise does not hold up under pressure. Real confidence comes from evidence: I tried, I improved, I handled that, I survived that, I came back, I can do hard things.

The parent's role is to help the athlete see that evidence without attaching worth to it.

The question parents should ask

At every age, ask: What kind of confidence does my athlete need right now? At eight, protect joy.

At twelve, protect willingness.

At fourteen, protect resilience.

At seventeen, protect identity.

Do not rush the stage. Do not demand adult confidence from a child. Do not mistake swagger for security.

The goal is not an athlete who never doubts.

The goal is an athlete who knows doubt is not the end of the story.

Chapter Tool

Confidence by Age Checklist

Age 8 — Joy
- [ ] Still wants to go

- [ ] Plays freely

- [ ] Laughs after mistakes

- [ ] Says "watch this"

- [ ] Feels safe trying

Age 12 — Willingness

- [ ] Tries hard things

- [ ] Accepts coaching

- [ ] Plays without needing perfection

- [ ] Handles comparison with support

- [ ] Still enjoys the sport

Age 14 — Resilience

- [ ] Bounces back from mistakes

- [ ] Does not define self by one game

- [ ] Understands growth is uneven

- [ ] Keeps working through awkward phases

- [ ] Can separate performance from identity

Age 17 — Identity

- [ ] Owns routines
- [ ] Communicates with coaches
- [ ] Handles setbacks with maturity
- [ ] Has interests beyond sport
- [ ] Knows they are more than an athlete

Chapter 13: Failure Is Information, Not a Verdict

Mistakes, Cuts, Slumps, Injuries, and Embarrassment
I was cut.

More than once.

I lead with that because people see the end of a story and assume the whole thing ran smooth. Drafted athlete. College coach. Advisor to families across a thousand kitchen tables. They don't see the earlier version — the young athlete who didn't make the team, who walked home angry, who lay awake wondering if he simply wasn't good enough. I was that kid. I know exactly what that ceiling feels like pressing down on you, because I lived under it.

And getting cut taught me something success never could have taught me as cleanly: nobody else was going to make me better. Not the coach who cut me, not my parents, not luck. Me. That lesson shaped the athlete, the coach, the father, and the man I became.

So I'm going to tell you the truth about failure that I learned the hard way, and it's not the truth you're expecting. The failure was never the problem. Failure is just information — neutral, useful, survivable. What turned my failures into either fuel or poison was never the cut itself.

It was what the adults around me did with it.

And that is the whole chapter. Because here is the thing no one says plainly enough: your child's failure is not a verdict. You are the one who decides whether it becomes one.

The two ways parents turn information into a verdict

When a child fails — gets cut, plays badly, loses the spot — the failure itself is neutral. It's a data point. It tells you something true about where they are right now. But most parents can't leave it neutral. The discomfort is too much, so we do something with it. And there are two moves we make, both meant to help, both quietly catastrophic.

The first is that we blame the world. The coach is an idiot. The official robbed us. It's politics, it's favoritism, it's the other family's money. And sometimes — let's be fair — some of that is even true; youth sports isn't always fair. But watch what you're teaching when you reach for it every single time: you are teaching your child that failure is always someone else's fault. You think you're protecting their confidence. You're actually stealing their power, because a child who believes nothing is ever their doing also believes nothing is ever in their control. You've handed them an excuse and called it loyalty, and excuses teach helplessness.

The second move is worse, and quieter, and almost no parent admits to it: we let the failure become who the child is. "You choked." "You embarrassed yourself out there." "You didn't want it enough." Maybe you'd never say those words — but your child reads the version you don't say, too. The silence in the car. The face that fell when they came off the field. The way you couldn't quite look at them the same that night. In that moment the child doesn't just experience a failure. They become one, in the eyes of the person whose eyes matter most. And shame doesn't teach effort. Shame teaches fear — fear of trying, fear of the next failure, fear of you.

Excuses or shame. Rescue or reject. Most of us, under the discomfort of watching our kid hurt, reach for one or the other without ever choosing it on purpose. And both take a neutral data point and stamp it into a verdict the child will carry for years.

The harder thing, and the only thing that works

There's a third option, and it's harder than either, which is exactly why it's rare. You let the failure stay what it actually is: information.

A mistake tells you what needs work. A cut tells you the athlete wasn't ready for that team, that level, that moment — yet. A slump tells you something about confidence or fatigue or approach. An injury tells you to look hard at workload and recovery. Embarrassment tells you the child cares, and gives you a chance to teach them how to come back without hiding. None of those are verdicts. Every one of them is a door, if a parent is steady enough to leave it open instead of slamming it shut with blame or shame.

But leaving it open costs you something, and I won't pretend it doesn't. It costs you the relief of doing something — fixing it, fighting it, explaining it away. It means sitting in your child's disappointment without rushing to end it, which is one of the most uncomfortable things a loving parent ever has to do. Your every instinct will scream to make the hurt stop. The discipline is to let it hurt, stay close, and trust that a child who learns "this hurt, and I survived it, and I was still loved through it" becomes someone almost impossible to break. A child who learns "this hurt, and my parent either rescued me or turned cold" walks into the next hard thing already afraid.

Sports hand you these chances over and over, while the stakes are still small — a missed shot at ten, a cut at thirteen, a slump at fifteen. Each one is a rehearsal for the genuinely hard things life will hand them at thirty, when you won't be in the stands. Don't waste the rehearsals by turning every one into a crisis. They are not crises. They are practice in being a person who can fail and rise — which is, in the end, the only skill that matters in any arena, long after the last whistle.

When the cut comes

Let me get specific, because the cut is the sharpest version of all of it.

When your child gets cut, your first job is not to explain it, fix it, fight it, or find the lesson. Your first job is to sit down next to them and let it hurt. Don't reach for the famous-athletes-who-got-cut speech. Don't promise they'll show everyone. Don't pull out your phone to draft a furious message to the coach. All of that is you managing your discomfort, not their pain. Just be there, in it, with them. Let them feel the whole weight of it, and let them feel you not leaving.

Then — later, after the emotion has drained off, maybe the next day — you ask the questions that hand them back the wheel. What did you learn? What feedback did you get? What do you want to do about it? Do you still want this? Those questions do something the blame and the shame never could: they return ownership to the athlete. They say, without saying it, this is yours, you can do something about it, and I believe you can. That's not coddling and it's not pressure. It's the exact middle that builds a person.

Slumps, injuries, and the steady parent

The same principle runs through all of it.

In a slump, the child already knows. They don't need you repeating the evidence after every game; they need a home where the slump doesn't become the whole family's mood. Are you sleeping? Eating enough? Enjoying any part of this? What's one small thing you can control tomorrow? Calm questions, quiet support, and the steady reminder that a slump is a chapter, not the book. The parent who panics over a slump teaches the child to panic. The parent who stays calm teaches the child that bad stretches are survivable — which is the whole lesson.

With injury — the hardest failure, because it takes away the very thing the child uses to feel capable — take the grief seriously; a sidelined kid can feel forgotten and useless. But hold the line on the one thing that actually matters: no game, no showcase, no roster spot is worth rushing a young body back before it's ready. The body comes first. Always. The adult who sacrifices a child's long-term health for a short-term event has confused the four-year plan for the forty-year one, and a child pays for that confusion in joints and confidence for decades.

The sentence to carry

So here is the line to keep, and to keep aimed at yourself before you aim it at your child:

Failure is information, not a verdict.

Say it after the mistakes, the cuts, the slumps, the injuries, the embarrassments. But understand what you're really promising when you say it. You're promising not to be the one who turns the information into a verdict. You're promising to sit in the discomfort instead of discharging it as blame or shame. You're promising that your child can fail in front of you — fully, publicly, repeatedly — and find that your love doesn't flicker, and that the failure is treated as a door and not a sentence.

I got cut, more than once, and it became fuel instead of poison for one reason: somewhere in there, the failure was allowed to stay information long enough for me to learn from it. That's the gift you can give your child every time they fall. Don't protect them from the hard feeling — they need the hard feeling. Protect them from the lie that the hard feeling is who they are.

Let failure teach. Never let it name them.

Chapter 14: Burnout Before It Becomes Obvious

How to Notice the Fade Before the Quit
Burnout almost never announces itself.

Your child is not going to walk into the kitchen one evening and say, clearly, "I think I'm burning out and I need you to help me." If only they would. It would be so much easier to respond to.

Instead, they fade.

That's the word I want you to carry out of this chapter. Fade. The child who used to grab their bag now leaves it by the door until you remind them. The one who used to narrate the whole game in the car goes quiet about the sport specifically. The laugh after practice gets shorter, then disappears. And then comes the one that should stop a parent cold: the day a canceled practice is met not with disappointment, but with relief.

Here is the gentle, difficult truth this chapter is built on, and I want to walk you toward it slowly because it's a hard thing to look at: most parents don't miss the fade because the signs are hidden. They miss it because the signs are inconvenient. We see them. We just explain them away — because the alternative is admitting something we don't want to admit.

The signs you've probably already seen

Let me ask you something, and I'd ask you to answer it honestly, even just to yourself.

When your child started dragging before practice — when "I'm tired" became the answer to everything — what did you tell yourself it was?

Most of us reach for the explanation that requires the least of us. They're just being lazy. It's a phase. They need to push through. Every athlete has off weeks. They'll snap out of it. And sometimes those explanations are even true. But sometimes — more often than we'd like — they're the story we tell ourselves so we don't have to hear the story the child is actually telling us with their slumped shoulders and their flat eyes and their relief when the gym closes.

I'm not saying that to make you feel guilty. I'm saying it because I have done it. I have looked at a tired, fading young person and reached for the explanation that let me keep the schedule intact, because the schedule was easier to protect than it was to question. Looking back is humbling. The signs weren't subtle. I just didn't want them to mean what they meant.

So here is the shift this chapter asks of you. Stop scanning your child for proof that everything's fine. Start being honest about the things you've already noticed and quietly filed away. Has the joy gone dim — not sad, just flat? Have they stopped talking about the sport? Has sleep changed, has mood changed around game days, have the friendships outside the sport thinned out? Are they relieved when it gets canceled? You probably didn't need this list. You could have written most of it yourself, about your own child, before you opened this chapter. The noticing was never the hard part. The admitting is.

"Lazy" is the most expensive word in youth sports

Of everything in this chapter, please hold onto this.

When a depleted child finally starts to fade — drags to practice, stops attacking the work, goes through the motions — the word that comes most easily to a frustrated parent is lazy. They've gotten lazy. They've lost their drive. They need to want it more.

I understand the word. I've felt the frustration behind it. But I have come to believe it's one of the most expensive words a parent can say, because it gets the child exactly backwards at the exact moment they most need to be understood.

A child who has been running year-round, through a schedule that would break most adults, who feels every game as a referendum on their worth and their future — that child is not lazy. That child is empty. And when you respond to emptiness with "you need to want it more," you are pouring demand into a tank that has nothing left to give, and calling the child a failure for running dry.

The depleted athlete does not need a motivational speech. They need a parent steady enough to set down their own disappointment and ask a different question. Not "why aren't you trying?" but "is this still good for you?" That question is hard to ask, because you might not like the answer, and the answer might cost you something you've invested years in. Ask it anyway. It is one of the few questions that can save both a child's love of the game and a child's relationship with you.

How the trap got built

Here's the part where I want to be careful, because I'm not here to tell you that you did this on purpose. No loving parent sits down and decides to burn their child out. The trap gets built one reasonable yes at a time.

The year-round commitment, because everyone serious does it now. The second team, because the first one wasn't enough. The private lessons, the speed training, the weekend that turns into a tournament that turns into a season with no edges. Each decision made out of love, each one defensible on its own. And then one day you have a child with no off-season, no unstructured afternoons, no stretch of time long enough to actually miss the thing they used to love — and you wonder why the spark went out.

Passion needs room to breathe. We have built a culture that gives children none, and then we diagnose the predictable result as a character flaw in the child. It isn't a character flaw. It's physics. A fire with no air goes out. That's not the child failing the sport. That's the adults around the child forgetting that a young person is not a machine you can run continuously and expect to keep loving the work.

When to pause — and why we're so afraid of it

When the signs cluster, the answer is often a pause. And I know that word frightens you, so let's be honest about why.

You're afraid a break will become a permanent quit. You're afraid the other kids will pass yours while you step back. You're afraid that resting is the same as falling behind. I understand all three fears. I've felt them.

But hear the difference: a planned pause is wisdom. A breakdown is the bill that comes due for ignoring the warning signs until the body or the spirit forces the issue. You will pause eventually. The only question is whether you choose the gentle version now or get handed the brutal version later.

A pause doesn't have to mean quitting. It can mean a week off. Skipping one event. Ending the second team. Taking a real off-season for the first time in years. Sometimes it means bringing in a professional — and I want to be clear and unembarrassed about this: if the warning signs cluster, if changes persist for weeks, if your child ever speaks of hopelessness or not wanting to be here, you involve a pediatrician or a licensed mental health professional, and you do it without shame. That is not an overreaction and it is not a failure. It is exactly what a good parent does. You are not equipped to diagnose your own child, and you were never supposed to be. Noticing is your job. Getting them to the right help is your job. The rest belongs to the professionals.

When they say the words

And sometimes, despite everything, your child will look at you and say it: I don't want to play anymore.

I need you to hear what I'm about to say, because this single moment determines more than almost any other in this book.

Do not panic. Do not argue. Do not list what you've spent — not the money, not the years, not the weekends. Do not say "but you love this." Do not make a tired child mount a legal defense of a feeling they can barely name themselves.

Because here is what's actually happening in that moment, underneath the words: your child is testing whether it's safe to tell you the truth. They have brought you the most honest, most vulnerable thing they have — and they are watching, in real time, to see what it costs them. If it costs them your warmth, your approval, a guilt trip about the investment, a frantic campaign to talk them out of it — they will learn the lesson instantly and permanently: don't bring the hard truths to this person. And they won't. Not about the sport, and eventually not about anything that matters.

So instead, get curious. "Tell me more." "Is it the sport, or is it this season?" "Is it the coach, the schedule, the pressure, your body, or something else?" "Do you want a break, or do you think you're really done?" You're not interrogating. You're showing them that their honesty is safe with you — which is, in the end, the only thing that keeps a child talking to a parent through adolescence and beyond.

And if it turns out they really are done? Then sit with this, because it matters: that is not the sport failing. If your child walks away having learned to compete, to lose, to work, to belong, to push their body and recover, to be part of something bigger than themselves — then the sport did its entire job, even if it ends at fourteen instead of in a stadium. You did not waste those years. You spent them well. The outcome was never a scholarship. The outcome was the person, and the person is right there in the passenger seat, still becoming.

What you're really protecting

So let me tell you what this chapter is actually about, underneath all the warning signs and the checklists.

You can survive your child leaving a sport. It might hurt. You might grieve a future you'd pictured. But you'll be fine, and so will they.

What's far harder to repair is a child who learned that you couldn't be trusted with the truth — who figured out, somewhere along the way, that their honesty made you anxious or angry or disappointed, and who quietly decided to stop giving it to you. That's the loss that lasts. Not the sport. The trust.

So when your child fades, when they drag, when they finally work up the courage to tell you they're done — meet it with steadiness, not panic. Make your home the one place where they can tell you a hard thing and watch your love not move an inch. Do that, and whatever happens with the sport, you'll have protected the thing that was always more important than any of it: a child who knows, all the way down, that they can come to you with the truth and still be completely loved.

That's the win. It always was.

Chapter 15: When the Pressure Gets Too Heavy

Mental Health, Anxiety, and Knowing When to Get Help

There are moments when sports pressure becomes too heavy for a young athlete to carry alone.

This is one of the most important chapters in the book, and it needs to be handled with care.

I am a coach. I am a parent. I have spent decades around athletes and families. But I am not a physician, therapist, psychologist, or licensed mental health professional. This book is not here to diagnose your athlete, and it should never be used that way.

This chapter is a flashlight.

It is here to help you notice.

It is here to help you ask better questions.

It is here to help you understand when the right move is not another practice, another speech, another lesson, or another push.

Sometimes the right move is help.

Pressure is not always bad

Not all pressure is harmful.

Healthy challenge is part of growth. Competition creates pressure. Tryouts create pressure. Hard games create pressure. Learning how to handle nerves, disappointment, criticism, and responsibility is one of the great values of sports.

A young athlete should not be protected from every uncomfortable feeling.

But there is a difference between challenge and overload.

Challenge stretches an athlete and leaves them stronger.

Overload crushes the athlete and leaves them smaller.

Challenge still has recovery, support, perspective, and safety around it.

Overload feels constant. It follows the athlete home. It enters sleep. It changes mood. It steals joy. It makes the sport feel like a threat.

Parents need to learn the difference.

What sport anxiety can look like

Anxiety in young athletes does not always sound like, "I am anxious."
It may look physical first.

Stomachaches before games. Headaches before practice. Trouble sleeping the night before competition. Needing the bathroom repeatedly before an event.

Shaking. Freezing. Going silent. Irritability. Anger. Tears that seem bigger than the moment.

Some athletes become perfectionistic. One mistake ruins the entire day. A missed shot, strikeout, turnover, fall, slow time, or bad shift becomes proof of something terrible.

Others go the opposite direction. They act like they do not care. They joke. They withdraw. They say, "Whatever." Sometimes "I do not care" means exactly that. Sometimes it means, "I care so much that it is safer to pretend I do not."

Parents must learn to read behavior, not just words.

Especially with teenagers.

When performance becomes identity

One of the greatest mental health risks in youth sports is when the athlete becomes only the athlete.

The sport becomes the whole house.

Every conversation is about the sport. Every weekend is about the sport. Every family mood depends on the sport. Every social media post centers the sport. Every compliment is tied to performance. Every future dream runs through the sport.

Then an injury, slump, benching, cut, or coach's decision does not feel like a setback.

It feels like an identity collapse.

That is dangerous.

A healthy athlete identity says:

"I love this sport. I work hard. I care deeply. But I am still a whole person if the sport goes badly."

An unhealthy athlete identity says:

"If I do not perform, I do not know who I am."

Parents have more power here than they realize. The way you talk at dinner matters. The way you introduce your athlete matters. The way your face changes after competition matters. The way you ask about school, friends, interests, rest, and feelings matters.

Make sure your athlete knows you see more than the uniform.

What parents should watch

Watch for patterns, not single bad days.

Every athlete has rough moments. A bad game can produce tears. A tough loss can create silence. A hard coach can cause frustration. A teenager can be moody because they are a teenager.

Do not panic over one day.

But do pay attention when changes persist.

Watch sleep. Appetite. Mood. School. Friendships. Energy. Motivation. Joy. Physical complaints. Isolation. Hopeless language. A loss of interest in things they used to enjoy. A fear of practice or games that seems disproportionate. Perfectionism that turns mistakes into emotional spirals. A sense that the athlete's entire worth has become tied to results.

Those are signals.

You do not need to know exactly what they mean to respond responsibly.

You only need to notice and act with care.

When to involve a professional

If concerning changes persist for weeks, involve help.
If the athlete mentions hopelessness, worthlessness, wanting to disappear, or not wanting to be here, involve help immediately.

If eating, sleep, mood, anxiety, injury, or identity concerns are beyond your ability to understand, involve help.

Start with a pediatrician, licensed mental health professional, school counselor, sports-medicine doctor, or qualified provider depending on the issue.

That is not overreacting.

That is parenting.

There is no trophy for handling serious concerns alone.

A parent's job is not to diagnose. A parent's job is to notice, stay calm, and get the right support.

What to say

If you are worried, begin with warmth.
Do not interrogate. Do not accuse. Do not say, "What is wrong with you?"

Try:

"I have noticed you seem different lately, and I care about you."

"You do not have to protect me from the truth."

"You are not in trouble."

"We can slow this down."

"You are more important than any team, season, or result."

"We will get help if we need it. That is not weakness."

The athlete needs to know that honesty will not cause panic or punishment.

If they believe telling the truth will make you angry, disappointed, or frantic, they may hide. And hiding is where problems grow.

The role of the parent

Your role is to create a home where the athlete can be more than their performance.

That means the relationship has to be bigger than the sport.

Ask about things that have nothing to do with competition. Notice effort in school. Notice kindness. Notice humor. Notice friendship. Notice courage outside the scoreboard. Let your athlete see that your pride is not tied only to visible success.

Keep family rhythms alive. Protect rest. Protect meals. Protect ordinary time. Make sure there are days where the athlete is not being evaluated, measured, filmed, corrected, or compared.

A young person cannot live inside evaluation all the time and remain healthy.

They need places where they are simply loved.

Home should be that place.

The final word on mental health

Sports can build resilience, confidence, discipline, friendship, and joy. Sports can also become too much.

Both truths are real.

The parent's job is to pay attention.

Not to panic.
Not to diagnose.

Not to toughen everything out.

Pay attention.

Ask.

Listen.

Get help when needed.

The athlete is the point.

Not the season. Not the roster. Not the scholarship. Not the reputation. Not the dream.

The athlete.

When the pressure gets too heavy, choose the athlete.

Every time.

Chapter Tool

Mental Health Parent Observation Sheet

This is not a diagnosis. Use it to notice patterns.
Over the last two to three weeks, have I noticed changes in:

- [ ] Sleep

- [ ] Appetite

- [ ] Mood

- [ ] School effort

- [ ] Friendships

- [ ] Energy

- [ ] Motivation

- [ ] Joy

- [ ] Physical complaints

- [ ] Anxiety before games or practices

- [ ] Perfectionism after mistakes

- [ ] Isolation

- [ ] Hopeless or worthless language

- [ ] Loss of interest in things beyond sport

If several are checked, start a calm conversation. If concerns persist, involve a qualified professional. If the athlete expresses hopelessness, worthlessness, self-harm thoughts, or not wanting to be here, seek immediate help.

Parent reminder: This book is a flashlight, not a doctor. Noticing is your job. Diagnosing is theirs.

Part IV — The Changing Athlete

Chapter 16: Build the Body, Don't Judge the Body

Puberty, Body Image, Strength, and Confidence

Puberty is the stage where a young athlete is most likely to either fall in love with their body or declare war on it.

That may sound strong, but I believe it is true. Between roughly twelve and seventeen, a young athlete's body changes faster than their confidence can always keep up. A girl may get stronger and more powerful, but also feel watched, compared, or uncomfortable in a body that no longer feels familiar. A boy may feel trapped in a body that has not grown yet while everyone around him seems bigger, faster, and stronger. An early bloomer may get attention too soon. A late bloomer may begin to believe they are behind for good.

And right in the middle of all of that are adults.

Parents. Coaches. Trainers. Teammates' parents. Social media. Ranking services. Highlight clips. Group chats. Weight-room chatter. Body comments disguised as coaching. Compliments that accidentally become pressure. Jokes that land harder than adults realize.

This is why the language around the changing athlete has to be handled carefully.

Words land deepest when the body is changing.

Choose them like they matter.

They do.

The body is not a verdict

One of the biggest mistakes adults make during puberty is treating a temporary body stage as a permanent athletic identity.

A boy who is small at thirteen is labeled limited. A girl whose body changes and movement feels awkward is treated like she is losing athleticism. An

early-maturing athlete is crowned too soon. A late-developing athlete is written off too early. A body becomes a verdict.

But the body at thirteen is not the body at seventeen.

The body at fourteen is not the body at twenty.

Puberty is not a fair race. It is staggered across years. Two athletes can be the same age on paper and live in completely different bodies. One may have adult strength and speed early. Another may still be waiting for the growth that will change everything. One may look powerful now and plateau later. Another may look awkward now and make a massive leap once coordination catches up.

Development is not linear.

It is a scribble, not a staircase.

Parents must stop turning the body into a final report card.

Building versus judging There is a difference between building the body and judging the body.

Building the body is forward-looking. It asks: what can this athlete learn to do? How can they get stronger? How can they move better? How can they stay healthy? How can they fuel the work? How can they recover? How can they become more capable?

Judging the body is verdict-based. It says: too small, too slow, too heavy, too thin, too bulky, not athletic enough, not strong enough, not fast enough, not like that other athlete.

Same body.

Opposite message.

Building creates ownership.

Judging creates shame.

This is especially important because young athletes will already compare themselves. They compare size, speed, strength, shape, skill, attention, ranking, social media, and body type. They do not need adults adding more comparison. They need adults helping them understand that their body is a tool to care for, fuel, strengthen, and trust — not an object to criticize.

What parents should say Talk about what the body can do, not how it looks.

Say:

"Look how much stronger you are getting."

"Your body is growing on its own schedule."

"Strength helps keep you healthy."

"What do you want your body to be able to do?"

"Let's fuel the work."

"That is their timeline. This is yours."

Do not say:

"You need to lose weight."

"You are getting bulky."

"Why do you look slower?"

"Why don't you look like them?"

"You are too small."

"You need to toughen up."

Even comments that seem harmless can get stored in a young athlete's mind for years.

A parent may say something once. The athlete may hear it for a decade.

What coaches and trainers must understand A coach or trainer who works with young athletes during puberty must understand age, stage, training age, growth, and confidence. They must know the difference between effort and exhaustion, between awkward growth and laziness, between healthy challenge and body shame.

If an environment regularly comments on bodies, weight, size, shape, or appearance, that is a red flag.

If athletes are compared publicly, weighed publicly, shamed publicly, or pressured to look a certain way, that is not development.

That is harm wearing a whistle.

The body should be discussed in terms of function, health, and capability. How does the athlete move? Are they strong enough for the demands of the sport? Are they fueling enough? Are they sleeping? Are they recovering? Are they safe?

That is the correct lane.

What the athlete needs during this stage The changing athlete needs five things.

First, they need patience. A body that changes quickly will not always perform smoothly. There may be clumsy phases, timing issues, strength imbalances, coordination dips, soreness, and confidence swings.

Second, they need fuel. A growing body that is also training needs enough food, enough hydration, enough sleep, and enough recovery.

Third, they need safe strength development. Strength is not punishment. Strength is not cosmetic. Strength is capability and protection when done correctly.

Fourth, they need language that anchors worth away from appearance and performance.

Fifth, they need adults who do not panic.

A calm parent can say: "This is real, and it is temporary. Your body is changing. We will be patient with it, fuel it, build it, and trust the process."

That sentence can steady an athlete more than another lesson ever will.

The one message every athlete needs Every athlete should hear this during puberty:

You are not behind. You are becoming. Your body is on its own clock and it is right on time. Fuel it, rest it, build it, be patient with it — and never forget that none of this changes how much I love you.

That is the message.

Not once.

Often.

Because the world will tell them to measure, compare, and judge.

Home should tell them the truth.

Chapter Tool

Build the Body, Don't Judge the Body — Language Swaps

Building Language	Judging Language
"Look how much more explosive you are."	"You would be faster if you dropped weight."
"Strength helps keep you healthy."	"You are getting bulky."
"What do you want your body to be able to do?"	"Why don't you look like them?"
"Your body is growing on its own schedule."	"You are behind."
"Let's fuel the work."	"Watch what you eat."
"That is their timeline. This is yours."	Comparing to a teammate or sibling.

Building talks about what the body does and will do. Judging talks about what the body is or looks like. Stay in the building lane.

Chapter 17: Female Athletes

Strength, Fueling, Confidence, REDs, and Body Trust
Female athletes are often carrying more pressure than adults realize.

They are expected to compete hard, train seriously, be confident, and perform under pressure. At the same time, many are also navigating body comparison, appearance pressure, social media, puberty, strength myths, nutrition confusion, and comments about their bodies that boys may not hear in the same way.

A female athlete's body is often evaluated twice.

What can it do?

And how does it look while doing it?

That second question can become heavy. It can make strength feel dangerous. It can make eating feel complicated. It can make a normal body change feel like a problem. It can make a powerful athlete begin to distrust the very body that is trying to help her become stronger.

Parents need to understand this clearly.

Strong is not the enemy.

Fuel is not the enemy.

Puberty is not the enemy.

The enemy is a culture that teaches a young female athlete to judge the body she needs to trust.

I have heard that culture come out of loving parents' mouths in a way that sounded harmless at first. A daughter begins strength training, and the first worry is not whether she will move better, stay healthier, or feel more confident. The first worry is whether she will get bulky. I understand where that fear comes from. Parents are hearing the same culture their daughters are hearing. But that sentence can do real damage, because it teaches a young female athlete to look at strength as a cosmetic risk instead of a protective gift.

I have watched strong girls absorb that message. They begin wondering whether training is changing how they look before they notice how much better they move. They start negotiating with the very body that is trying to help them become more durable, more powerful, and more confident. That is why parents have to be so careful here. A daughter does not need adults making strength sound suspicious. She needs adults helping her trust the body she is building.

Strength is protection One of the most important messages parents can give a female athlete is this:

Strength helps keep you on the field, court, rink, track, mat, pool deck, or course.

Strength is not about looking a certain way. It is about capability. It is about durability. It is about learning to land, cut, accelerate, decelerate, absorb contact, hold posture, repeat movement, and stay healthy through the demands of sport.

Too many girls still hear the old lie that strength training will make them "bulky" or less feminine or somehow wrong. Parents should kill that myth early.

Strong is the goal.

Strong helps protect the athlete.

Strong gives confidence.

Strong is not a cosmetic project.

When you talk about strength with a daughter, keep the language functional:

"You are moving better."

"You look more stable."

"You are getting more powerful."

"Your body is learning how to protect you."

Avoid appearance language. Avoid weight language. Avoid comparisons. Avoid comments that make the athlete feel observed instead of supported.

Fuel is part of training The danger for many hardworking female athletes is not eating too much.

It is under-fueling.

Under-fueling means the athlete is not eating enough to support growth, training, competition, school, recovery, hormones, and normal life. Sometimes it is intentional. Sometimes it is accidental. Sometimes the athlete is simply busy. Sometimes the culture has quietly taught her that eating less is somehow better.

The body does not care why the fuel is missing. It only knows that it does not have enough.

When a young athlete trains hard and does not fuel enough, the body begins to protect itself. Recovery suffers. Mood changes. Energy drops. Injuries can pile up. Performance may plateau or slide. Bone health can be affected. Menstrual health can be affected. Confidence can be affected.

This is why food must be normalized.

Not moralized.

Food is not good or bad. Food is fuel. Food is recovery. Food is growth. Food is the material the body uses to adapt to training.

Parents do not need to turn the kitchen into a laboratory. But they do need to make sure the athlete is eating enough, eating regularly, hydrating, and recovering.

If eating becomes stressful, rigid, secretive, or tied to fear, bring in qualified help. A pediatrician, sports-medicine physician, or registered dietitian can help guide the family.

Do not guess with a young athlete's body.

Menstrual health matters A regular menstrual cycle is a health signal.

A missed, irregular, or lost period in a hardworking athlete should not be dismissed as "normal for athletes" or "just training hard." It may be a sign that the body is under stress, under-fueled, or not recovering well.

Parents do not need to panic. But they do need to notice and involve the right professional.

This is not a shame conversation.

It is a health conversation.

The tone matters. A daughter should not feel accused, blamed, or embarrassed. She should feel supported.

Try:

"This is information your body is giving us. We are not mad. We are going to get the right support."

That kind of language protects trust.

Puberty and performance Puberty can temporarily make a female athlete feel worse at her sport.

New height. New center of gravity. New strength. New movement patterns. A body that suddenly handles differently. Timing can feel off. Speed can change. Coordination can dip. Confidence can wobble.

This does not mean she is losing it.

It means her body is changing and her skills need time to catch up.

The worst thing adults can do is panic during that phase. Do not pile on extra training to fix what may simply be a temporary adjustment. Do not compare

her to her younger self. Do not comment on how her body has changed. Do not let her believe becoming a young woman made her less athletic.

Be steady.

Say:

"Your body is changing. That is normal. We will keep building, keep fueling, keep resting, and let your skills catch up."

That is the message.

What a healthy environment looks like A strong female athlete environment celebrates capability.

It talks about what bodies do, not how they look. It normalizes food. It treats strength as protection. It does not comment on weight or shape. It supports rest and recovery. It understands menstrual health. It trains landing, cutting, movement quality, and strength responsibly. It makes athletes feel powerful, not watched.

If a program comments on girls' bodies, uses weight as motivation, dismisses missed periods, encourages restriction, or treats shame as toughness, parents should pay close attention.

That is not an elite environment.

That is a dangerous one.

What every female athlete should hear Your body is doing exactly what it is supposed to do.

Strong is the goal.

You are not a project to fix.

You are not a number.

You are not less because your body is changing.

You are becoming stronger, and we are going to fuel, rest, and support that process.

Nothing your body does or does not do changes how loved you are.

Say it before she needs it.

Say it again after.

Chapter Tool

Under-Fueling / REDs Parent Watch List

This is not a diagnosis. It is a reason to notice, stay calm, and seek qualified help.

Watch for patterns over weeks.

- [ ] Periods become irregular, lighter, or stop
- [ ] Stress fractures
- [ ] Injuries pile up or heal slowly
- [ ] Fatigue that rest does not fix
- [ ] Getting sick more often
- [ ] Eating less while training more

- [ ] Noticeable weight loss

- [ ] Always cold

- [ ] Hair or skin changes

- [ ] Performance sliding despite more effort

- [ ] Flat mood or irritability

- [ ] Anxiety around food

- [ ] Rigid food rules

- [ ] Skipping meals

Two or more signs, or any menstrual change: stay warm, keep it low-drama, and contact a pediatrician, sports-medicine physician, or registered dietitian.

This is a "we are going to get you support" moment, not a "what are you doing to yourself" moment.

Chapter 18: Male Athletes

Size, Speed, Toughness, Late Growth, and Hidden Anxiety
For many male athletes, puberty feels like a public ranking system.

Who is biggest? Who is fastest? Who is strongest? Who throws hardest? Who hits farthest? Who dunks first? Who gets attention? Who looks like a varsity athlete before everyone else?

That becomes the currency.

And for the late-developing boy, it can feel brutal.

He may be doing everything right. He may love the sport. He may have skill, feel, instincts, and work ethic. But at thirteen or fourteen, the athlete who matured earlier can simply overpower him. The early bloomer wins on size. The late bloomer wonders if he is falling behind.

Parents need to be careful here.

A boy may not say he is embarrassed.

He may not say he feels small.

He may not say he is scared the game is passing him.

He may say, "I am fine."

And he may say it through clenched teeth.

I've watched this story play out so many times that I want to tell you about three young men at once — not because their sport matters, but because their path does. They happen to be baseball players I've known since 2011, all from the same corner of Louisiana. But before you decide this is a baseball story, hear me: I have seen this exact thing in gyms and pools and on soccer pitches and wrestling mats. Swap the sport and the details, and it is the same story every time. Here it is.

All three of these boys were written off by their own high school coaches. Not one was a high school standout. And all three became NCAA Division I starting athletes. The only thing that separated who they became from who their coaches assumed they were was time, work, and the right environment — the three things the late-developing athlete needs most and is most often denied.

Mason was, in his own words, basically the pinch runner at his high school — maybe twenty or thirty innings in the field across his whole career. Hardly anyone believed he could play at a high level; his own coaches told him he was a great fielder who simply couldn't hit. But Mason had something real underneath the thin résumé: elite speed, genuine outfield ability, and enough belief to keep working while everyone else was busy deciding what he was. He needed time and a plan, and a postgraduate year gave him the runway. He kept building his body, kept working on the bat, and Northeastern became the right fit. He started four years there, played two summers in the Cape Cod League against future big leaguers, and won a Silver Slugger. The kid who couldn't hit.

Darren I remember best for his work ethic — he was in my facility constantly, him and his dad, hitting for hours whether he had practice or not. His high school coach told me, to my face, that I was selling dollars and dreams. His exact words were: If he can't hit at the high school level, how can he possibly hit at the college level? I'm sure that coach cared about Darren. He just couldn't see him. Darren went on to be a four-year starter at the University of New Orleans — and one of only about twenty-three players in NCAA Division I history to hit two grand slams in a single game. He did it by doing the least dramatic thing in sports: showing up the same way on good days and bad days, and refusing to take no for an answer.

Caleb took the path nobody applauds in the moment. He was a center fielder who could chase down anything but struggled at the plate, so we talked about a position change to pitcher to match his arm. Then came Tommy John surgery that wiped out a senior year and most of a college freshman year, a transfer to junior college that everyone questioned, and years of grinding before it broke his way. He was drafted, and he's pitched all the way to Triple-A. Caleb is the one who taught me a line I've never forgotten. He refused to run on bitterness. I don't try to prove everyone wrong, he told me. I try to prove the people who believed in me right. Read that twice. It's the healthiest fuel an athlete can run on, and most never find it.

Three boys. A pinch runner, a kid who couldn't hit, and an outfielder who had to become a pitcher. Three coaches who couldn't see them. Three Division I careers anyway. The lesson is not that every overlooked kid becomes one of these three — they won't, and selling that is its own kind of lie. The lesson is simpler and truer: an athlete can have a tool, a weakness, a timeline, and a future all at the same time. Parents panic when one piece is missing. Development waits long enough to build the missing piece. And if you remember one thing from this chapter, let it be the thing I told all three of them, the thing that turned out to be the whole story of their careers: it's not how you start. It's how you finish.

He needed time. He needed a plan. He needed the right environment. A postgraduate year helped give him that runway. He kept developing physically, kept working on his bat, and eventually Northeastern became the right fit. He went on to play four years there, spend two summers in the Cape Cod League, and win a Silver Slugger award. The lesson is not that every late bloomer becomes Mason. The lesson is that an athlete can have a tool, a weakness, a timeline, and a future all at the same time. Parents panic when one piece is missing. Development waits long enough to build the missing piece.

The toughness trap Male athletes are often taught a narrow version of toughness.

Do not show pain. Do not show fear. Do not admit doubt. Do not cry. Do not be soft. Do not ask for help. Do not let anyone see that something hurt you.

That code does not make boys stronger.

It often makes them lonelier.

A boy who is struggling may hide it through anger, sarcasm, withdrawal, jokes, or the classic line: "I do not care."

Sometimes he does care. He cares so much that pretending not to care feels safer than trying and being embarrassed.

Parents need to read behavior, not just words.

If a male athlete suddenly becomes irritable, shuts down, avoids practice, mocks the sport, says he does not care, or seems angry after every game, do not immediately assume attitude. Ask what is underneath.

Anger is often the emotion boys are allowed to show when the real emotion is fear, shame, disappointment, or sadness.

Make it safe for him to tell the truth.

Late bloomers need protection and patience A late-developing male athlete at thirteen or fourteen needs one thing above all: belief that is not based on current size.

Do not minimize how hard it is. Do not simply say, "You will grow." He is living in the body he has right now. He is being compared right now. He is losing reps right now. He is getting outmuscled right now.

A better message is:

"This stage is hard, and I see that. Your body is on its own timeline. Our job is to keep building skill, strength, confidence, and habits while your body catches up."

Late bloomers often develop things early bloomers never had to develop: skill, creativity, patience, toughness, feel, and work ethic. They learn to compete without overwhelming physical advantages. Then, when the body finally catches up, those skills remain.

That is why parents should protect them through the gap.

Keep them in environments that develop skill, not just reward size. Keep them multi-sport if possible. Make sure they are playing, learning, and staying confident. Get them around coaches who understand development and do not write off late bloomers.

The wrong environment can make a late bloomer quit before the body arrives.

Do not let that happen.

Early bloomers need humility and challenge The early-developing male athlete has a different risk.

He may get praised too soon for things that are not yet skill. He may dominate because he is bigger, stronger, or faster, not because he has built the complete game. Adults may crown him early. Parents may believe the future is already obvious. Coaches may ride his physical advantage for wins.

That can be dangerous.

Early size is a temporary loan, not a permanent gift.

If the early bloomer never learns skill, discipline, coachability, humility, and resilience, he may struggle when everyone else catches up. And eventually, many do catch up.

Parents of early bloomers should praise work, not size.

Do not say, "You are just bigger than everyone."

Say, "I like how you prepared." "I like how you competed." "I like how you handled that correction." "I like how you made your teammate better."

Make sure the athlete is challenged. Make sure they are not only dominating weaker competition. Make sure they learn to lose, adjust, and be coached.

If an early bloomer never struggles until the stakes are high, the struggle may break them.

Let them struggle while the stakes are still low.

Numbers are snapshots, not destiny Parents can become obsessed with measurables.

Velocity. Forty times. Vertical jumps. Bench press numbers. Sprint times. Rankings. Size. Weight. Strength. Speed.

Those numbers can be useful. They can help track development. They can reveal progress. They can motivate training.

But at thirteen or fourteen, many numbers are simply a snapshot of puberty.

They are not destiny.

A young athlete's number today may tell you where their body is in the maturation process. It may not tell you who they will become.

Chasing numbers too early can cause problems. Throwing too hard too young, lifting too heavy before technique is ready, chasing speed without movement quality, training for optics instead of development — these can all put the athlete at risk.

Develop the athlete.

Do not chase the number.

The number is a weather report.

You are raising a climate.
What every male athlete should hear You are growing on your own clock.

That clock is not behind anyone else's.

I am proud of how you work, how you treat people, how you compete, and who you are right now — this size, this speed, this stage.

You do not have to be tough for me.

You have to be honest with me.

If something hurts, say it.

If you are scared, say it.

If you are embarrassed, say it.

That honesty is not weakness.

It is maturity.

A boy who hears that at home can stop pretending long enough to grow.

Chapter Tool

Male Athlete Puberty Message Card

Say often:
• "You are growing on your own clock."

• "You are not behind."

• "I am proud of your work and your character, not just your size or speed."

• "You do not have to be tough for me. You can be honest with me."

• "Develop the athlete. Do not chase the number."

• "The body will change. The habits you build now will stay."

Avoid:
• "You need to get bigger."

• "Why are you so small?"

• "Stop being soft."

• "You should be faster by now."

• Comparing his body or numbers to a teammate, sibling, or parent.

Chapter 19: Strength, Conditioning, Nutrition, Sleep, and Recovery

When the Habits Become Serious
Parents often ask the wrong version of the question.

They ask, "When should my athlete start training?"

The better question

is, "What kind of training matches my athlete's age, stage, body, and readiness?"
Because the habits matter early.

The intensity should arrive later.

That is the order many families get wrong.

They professionalize the child before the child has built a foundation. They add adult-style training to a young body that needs movement, play, sleep, food, and variety. They chase speed, strength, velocity, power, rankings, and physical numbers before the athlete understands how to move well.

Strength and conditioning can be extremely valuable when done correctly.

Done too early, too intensely, or by the wrong person, it becomes another way adults rush the process.

Ages 6-9: movement and joy At ages six through nine, the training program should not look like training.

It should look like play.

Run. Jump. Skip. Climb. Throw. Catch. Balance. Roll. Tumble. Swim. Ride a bike. Play tag. Play different sports. Move in every direction. Learn where the body is in space.

That is physical development.

A child this age does not need sport-specific strength training. They do not need speed packages. They do not need adult-style workouts. They need a broad movement foundation and a body that loves to move.

Nutrition at this age should be simple: enough food, mostly real food, water, family meals when possible, and no food fear.

Sleep is the performance program.

A tired eight-year-old does not need another lesson.

They need bedtime.

Ages 10-12: skill and movement quality At ages ten through twelve, athletes can begin learning movement patterns more intentionally.

Squat. Hinge. Lunge. Land. Brace. Change direction. Decelerate. Balance. Coordinate. Move with control.

This still does not have to mean heavy weights or intense specialization. It means learning how to move before loading movement.

This is a good age for bodyweight strength, medicine-ball games, coordination, mobility, jumping and landing mechanics, sprint games, and structured play that teaches athletic movement without turning the athlete into a mini-professional.

Nutrition becomes a little more intentional: breakfast matters, hydration matters, snacks matter, enough food matters. The athlete should begin understanding that food helps the body do work.

Sleep still wins more games than parents realize.

At this age, protect multi-sport participation as long as possible. Different sports build different physical qualities. A soccer season, basketball season, swim season, lacrosse season, softball season, track season, football season, tennis season, or volleyball season can each develop the body in different ways.

Variety builds the athlete.

Ages 13-14: the hinge years At thirteen and fourteen, strength, conditioning, nutrition, sleep, and recovery begin to matter in a more serious way.

This does not mean the athlete should train like a college player.

It means the athlete is entering a stage where the body is changing quickly, competition is increasing, injury risk can rise, and habits begin to separate athletes.

This is where a qualified strength coach can become valuable.

Qualified matters.

Not every adult with a whistle and a weight room understands young athletes. Parents should ask about certification, experience with adolescents, injury philosophy, movement assessment, and how the program handles growth spurts, fatigue, and multi-sport athletes.

Safe training at this age is built on technique first. Light loads. Supervision. Quality movement. No ego lifting. No max-out culture. No social media workouts. No copying college or professional programs.

Training age matters more than birthday age. A fourteen-year-old who has never trained starts at the beginning. That is not weakness. That is intelligence.

Nutrition becomes serious because the body is growing and training. Under-fueling becomes a real risk. A growing athlete who does not eat enough cannot recover, adapt, or stay healthy.

Sleep becomes non-negotiable.

Recovery becomes part of the program.

A thirteen-year-old who is always sore, always tired, always injured, or always flat is not becoming tougher.

They may be under-recovered.

Ages 15-17: build the athlete At fifteen through seventeen, structured strength and conditioning can become a major part of development if the athlete is ready and supervised properly.

This is where progressive training can help build strength, speed, power, durability, confidence, and ownership. But the principles do not change.

Technique before load.

Quality before ego.

Recovery before more volume.

Food and sleep before supplements.

Consistency before intensity.

The older athlete must begin owning habits. They should know their sleep matters. They should pack food. They should hydrate. They should understand warm-ups, cooldowns, mobility, recovery, and how their body feels. They should track energy, mood, and soreness. They should begin understanding that a serious athlete does not just train hard.

A serious athlete recovers hard.

The priority order Here is the order I want parents to remember:

Sleep first.

Food second.

Training third.

Almost everyone has it upside down.

They chase a trainer before they fix bedtime. They buy supplements before they build meals. They add workouts before they ask whether the athlete is recovering from the current workload.

You cannot out-train a tired, under-fueled athlete.

You cannot outwork bad recovery forever.

The most underrated performance program in America is a regular bedtime, enough food, and a sane schedule.

That may not sell as well as a speed program or a showcase package.

But it works.

The parent standard Do not professionalize the body before the athlete is ready.

Do not ignore strength and recovery when the athlete becomes ready.

Both mistakes matter.

The younger athlete needs movement, joy, variety, sleep, and food.

The middle-school athlete needs patience, safe movement instruction, fueling, recovery, and gradual ownership.

The high-school athlete needs structure, progressive training, sleep discipline, nutrition, and accountability.

At every stage, the goal is the same:

Build a healthy, durable, confident athlete who can keep playing.

Not just this weekend.

For the long game.

Ages 10-16: Prepare, Don't Panic Ages ten through sixteen are not a recruiting emergency.

They are a preparation window.

From ten to twelve, build fun, foundation, fundamentals, repetition, movement, confidence, and love of play.

From twelve to fourteen, watch growth, maturity, learning style, travel-program fit, and the athlete's ability to learn through healthy competition.

From fourteen to sixteen, begin preparing the athlete for what older competition asks: strength, recovery, sport IQ, execution, mental discipline, body awareness, nutrition, sleep, and responsibility.

There is nothing urgent between ages ten and sixteen with regard to college recruiting.

There is plenty that matters.

The difference matters.

Play More Catch, Throw More Often, Pitch Less

For throwing athletes, arm care is not only about the arm.

It is the whole body. Feet, legs, hips, trunk, shoulder, elbow, wrist, fingers, recovery, strength, mobility, and timing all work together.

Parents often chase velocity too early because velocity is easy to measure and easy to sell. But young athletes need accuracy, movement, healthy throwing volume, proper progression, body control, recovery, and full-body strength before they need velocity programs.

Play more catch. Throw more often. Pitch less.

That simple idea protects the difference between throwing as healthy development and pitching as the higher-stress version of throwing. A young athlete should learn to move their feet, throw accurately, use the body, recover, and recognize fatigue before adults chase radar-gun numbers.

Velocity should not become a childhood scoreboard.

Build the body first. Teach the movement. Protect recovery. Let strength and speed develop responsibly.

The body will only allow what it can decelerate and recover from.

Chapter Tool

Sleep-Food-Training Priority Check

Before adding more training, ask:
1. Is my athlete sleeping enough?

2. Is my athlete eating enough?

3. Is my athlete hydrating consistently?

4. Is my athlete recovering between sessions?

5. Is the current workload already too heavy?

6. Is this training age-appropriate?

7. Is the coach qualified to train adolescents?

8. Is technique being taught before load?

9. Is the athlete getting stronger, or just more tired?

10. Are we building durability, or chasing numbers?

Priority order: Sleep first. Food second. Training third.

Chapter 20: Fuel the Work

Tournament Weekends, Energy, Recovery, and Under-Fueling

Tournament weekends expose the truth about a family — not the athlete's talent, the family's habits. What does the kid eat? When do they sleep? How do they recover? How many hours in the car, how many games stacked into one day, how do they hold up when they're tired, hungry, hot, and running on nothing?

Here's the uncomfortable math most families never do out loud. We will spend thousands of dollars to get a child into a competitive environment — the team, the travel, the hotel, the registration — and then treat the fuel and the rest that let them actually compete in it as an afterthought, something we'll figure out at the concession stand. We pour money into the opportunity and pocket change into the body that has to seize it. That's backwards. If the body is the vehicle, food and sleep aren't details. They're the engine. You wouldn't drive a car three states to a race and forget to put gas in it. We do exactly that to our kids most weekends and then wonder why they sputter by Sunday.

The simplest message there is

You don't need to turn nutrition into a science project. The whole message is two words: fuel the work. A child who is training, competing, growing, studying, and traveling needs enough fuel to do all of it — and a growing athlete often needs far more than a parent expects, because the body is doing two jobs at once, building a person and performing a sport.

Under-fueling can happen to any athlete, in any sport, on purpose or by pure accident — the skipped breakfast, the nerves that kill an appetite, the no-time-between-games, the quiet cultural message that eating less is somehow discipline. The body doesn't care why the fuel is missing. It only knows it's short, and it starts shutting things down to cope: recovery slows, mood flattens, injuries pile up, performance slides. A tired, flat, frequently hurt athlete usually doesn't need more desire. They need more food, more sleep, and more recovery — and a parent honest enough to consider that before reaching for "you need to want it more."

Tournament reality, and the trap inside it

Let me take you to a Sunday afternoon I've watched more times than I can count.

I think again of that same family, because the nutrition piece changed more than the body. When the father first started looking honestly at what his son was eating, he realized what so many parents realize: the athlete was not fueled for the amount of school, training, growing, and competing he was being asked to carry. The answer was not complicated. It was consistent.

At first, the family had to learn when the boy could actually eat. For him, the window was right after school, so his father made sure there was real food waiting — burritos, tacos, peanut butter and jelly, noodles, whatever gave him enough energy to recover from the day and prepare for the work ahead. Over time the athlete began to take ownership. He learned to cook. Breakfast became serious: eggs, toast, fruit, a smoothie, enough food before school that his body had something to build with instead of something to survive on.

And the payoff was not only weight on a scale or numbers in a weight room. His energy changed. His confidence changed. His willingness to work changed. Even the household changed. The same athlete learning to fuel himself was also learning to manage school, routines, laundry, and responsibility. Food became part of maturity. That is the point parents miss: fueling the work is not just about performance. It is one of the first ways a young athlete learns to take care of the life they are trying to build.

Nothing was wrong with that athlete's heart. Everything was wrong with the conditions we'd put them in — and then graded them against.

Tournament weekends are often built in ways that would wreck an adult, let alone a growing kid. Early wake-ups, long drives, hotel sleep, whatever food is nearby, heat and cold, back-to-back games with sitting in between, emotional highs and lows, a stressed parent in the front seat. And then — this is the part that should stop you — the adults evaluate the performance as if the child were operating under normal conditions. They are not. You cannot starve a kid of food, sleep, and recovery for forty-eight hours and then read the fourth-game slump as a character flaw. That's not a scouting report. That's a fuel gauge on empty, and you're the one who didn't fill the tank.

A good plan doesn't guarantee a good performance, but it protects the child from breaking down for no reason. Plan the food before you leave. Pack what they'll actually eat. Build hydration into the day. Protect sleep where you can. Keep the car calm and resist turning every gap between games into a film session. And understand that a kid wrecked by the end of a long weekend isn't weak. That's physiology, and pretending otherwise just teaches them to distrust their own body.

What to eat, the supplement trap, and recovery

Keep it practical. Before competition: fuel they can digest — carbs for energy, some protein, familiar foods, nothing experimental on game day. Across a long day: regular small refuels — fruit, sandwiches, yogurt, rice bowls, wraps, bars that agree with them, water, electrolytes when heat and sweat justify it. After: food, fluids, and sleep, which does the deepest repair of all. The exact meal matters less than the pattern — eat enough, eat often, hydrate, recover. Do not let a young athlete run an entire day on caffeine, sugar, and adrenaline.

And one thing said plainly, because the industry is loud here: most young athletes do not need energy drinks, stimulant products, or a supplement routine scraped off social media. They need food, water, sleep, and consistency. If a supplement is genuinely being considered, that's a conversation with a physician or registered dietitian — not an influencer, who can be wrong, sponsored, or both, and who has never once met your child. Food first. Sleep first. Real professional guidance when needed. Don't let someone with a discount code become your kid's nutritionist.

Recovery, finally, is not laziness — it's when the body actually absorbs the work. The athlete who never recovers doesn't bank the training; they just accumulate fatigue and call it commitment. Recovery is sleep, food, hydration, lighter days, real rest days, and time away from being evaluated. It's emotional too: after a long weekend, a kid often doesn't need a performance breakdown. They need a shower, a meal, sleep, and quiet. The strongest athletes aren't the ones who can tolerate the most chaos. They're the ones who learned to prepare, fuel, recover, and repeat — while the families who confused exhaustion with dedication slowly wore their kids out and never understood why the fire went cold.

Chapter Tool

Tournament Fuel and Recovery Planner

Before: Know the schedule. Plan meals before you travel. Pack snacks the athlete actually eats. Bring water and real hydration. Protect the night-before sleep. No new foods or supplements on game day.

During: Eat breakfast. Refuel between games. Hydrate on a schedule. Manage heat and cold. Keep breaks calm, not lectures. Watch for fatigue, irritability, dizziness, or unusual flatness.

After: A recovery meal. Rehydrate. Sleep. Let the athlete decompress before any evaluation.

Parent reset: Fuel the work. Protect recovery. And never again confuse an empty tank with a weak heart.

Part V — The Youth Sports Machine

Chapter 21: Who Gets Access to Your Athlete?

Coaches, Programs, Trust, and the Adults You Let Shape Your
Child You are about to give a stranger enormous power over your child.
Their confidence, their body, their relationship with a sport they love,
sometimes their whole sense of whether they're any good. We hand that power
over casually — sign up, pay the fee, drop them off — and then act surprised
when it goes wrong.

It doesn't have to be a gamble. You can read a coach and read a program
before you commit, the same way you'd read any person you were about to trust
your athlete to. Here's how.

One thing to know going in: youth sports has a quiet structural problem.
There's no real licensing, no systematic training requirement, no oversight for
most of the adults coaching American athletes. The travel-and-club

economy that's grown into a multi-billion-dollar business — where the
average family now spends over a thousand dollars a year on one sport — runs
largely on adults who appointed themselves. Some are gifted and selfless. Some
are selling you fear and calling it development. The fee tells you nothing about
which one you've got. So you have to learn to tell the difference yourself. That's
the whole chapter.

1. What should parents look for in a coach at each age? The mistake parents
make is using the same checklist at every age. What a great coach does for an
eight-year-old and what a great coach does for a sixteen-year-old are almost
opposite jobs. Match the coach to the stage.

Ages 6-9 — The coach's only real job is to make them love it and want to
come back. At this age, retention is the entire game. Remember that most
athletes quit by thirteen — and the coach who makes six-year-olds dread
practice is the front end of that statistic. Look for warmth, patience, and
energy. Look for a coach who gives every athlete real reps and real playing time,
teaches the basics through play, and laughs a lot. The ratio you're measuring
isn't wins-to-losses. It's smiles per practice. A great 6-9 coach could lose every
game and be doing a perfect job, because the job is planting joy. Run from any
coach at this age who cares about the scoreboard, benches little athletes to win,
runs up scores, or already has "favorites." A coach treating eight-year-olds like a
competitive asset is a coach to walk away from, no matter how many trophies
are in the case.

Ages 10-12 — The coach's job shifts to teaching the game and building skill
plus ownership. Now you want someone who genuinely teaches —
fundamentals, the "why" behind them, how to read the game — while keeping
it fun. Look for a coach who develops the whole roster, not just the three early-
bloomers who are big for their age. Look for one who communicates with
families, supports multi-sport athletes, and isn't pushing year-round
specialization. The tell of a bad 10-12 coach is that playing time tracks size and
early puberty instead of effort and growth — they're riding the athletes who

matured first and ignoring the ones who'll be better at sixteen. That coach is mortgaging your late bloomer's future for a U12 banner.

Ages 13-14 — The hinge years, and the coach's job is to develop athletes through chaos without crushing them. This is the hardest coaching stage and the one that separates the real ones. Bodies are exploding and falling

apart at the same time — the growth spurt wrecks coordination, spikes injury risk, and tanks confidence right when social pressure peaks. The coach you want has patience with the awkward phase, understands that a suddenly-clumsy athlete grew three inches and isn't regressing, and keeps developing the athlete who's temporarily worse. Look for individual development, honesty delivered with care, and someone who's a safe base while starting real accountability. The red flag here is brutal and common: the coach who writes off late bloomers, plays only the early-matured athletes, and treats thirteen-year-olds like professionals. That coach culls your athlete right before the growth spurt that would've made them good.

Ages 15-17 — The coach's job is to prepare them for what's next — as an athlete and a person — honestly. Now you want honesty above almost everything. A great coach at this age tells the truth about where the athlete actually stands, holds high standards with respect, develops them in a way that prepares them to be coached by someone else at the next level, and treats them like the near-adults they are. The best ones reinforce the 40-year frame — they care about the athlete's grades, their character, their life past the final whistle. The danger at this stage is the coach who oversells: false scholarship promises, exposure hype, burning athletes out chasing a title for the program's reputation, dishonesty about fit because the truth is inconvenient. A coach using your seventeen-year-old as a billboard for their own program is not preparing your athlete. They're spending them.

2. The clearest red flags in a coach You can usually spot a bad coach inside two practices if you know what you're watching for. The clearest red flags: • They motivate through fear, shame, and humiliation — and call it toughness. If your athlete is smaller after practice instead of tired- but-lit-up, that's the tell. • Athletes are afraid of them, not just respectful. There's a world of difference, and athletes' body language shows it. • Favoritism unrelated to effort or merit — politics, money, last name, or whose dad helps the program. • They oversell. Promises about scholarships, exposure, "the next level." A coach trafficking in guarantees is selling, not developing. • They won't be questioned. A reasonable parent question gets treated as betrayal. Defensiveness is information.

• They talk about themselves more than the athletes. Their record, their connections, their reputation — the athlete is a prop in the coach's story. • They're inconsistent — a different person when they're winning than when they're losing. Athletes can't feel safe on a roller coaster. • They have zero interest in the athlete as a person — only as a piece on the board. • They encourage overuse, specialization, or playing hurt. A coach who wants your athlete to skip the off-season, drop other sports, or "push through" an injury is prioritizing the program's wins over your child's body. Unforgivable.

Any one of these is a yellow flag. Two or three together, and the trophies don't matter — get your athlete out.

3. The clearest green flags in a coach The good ones share a signature, and once you've seen it you can't unsee it. A great coach is demanding and warm at the same time — high standards, high care, no contradiction between them. The specific green flags: • Athletes want to be around them. They leave practice tired but lifted. That's the master signal. • They teach the "why," not just the drill — they're building understanding, not obedience. • They develop the whole roster, and coach the bottom of the bench as hard as the top. • They're honest even when it's hard, and they don't oversell. A coach who'll tell you a truth you don't want is a coach you can trust with the truths you do. • They care about the athlete as a person — the grades, the mood, the life outside the lines. • They're consistent — the same human win or lose, so athletes can take risks without fear. • They welcome reasonable questions and are transparent about how decisions get made. • They develop athletes out of needing them — the highest form of coaching, preparing an athlete to succeed at the next level, under the next coach, without them.

• They manage bodies responsibly — rest, recovery, multi-sport room, and they never want an athlete playing hurt.

The one-line test, same as the program test: a great coach makes your athlete braver. A bad coach makes your athlete more afraid.

4. What a development-first program looks like A development-first program can articulate what it's actually doing — and what it says holds up when you watch. The markers: • A real philosophy, not just a schedule. Ask "how do you develop a player here" and you get a clear answer about how athletes get better, not a pitch about showcases and connections. • Everyone develops, not just the studs. The athlete in the middle of the roster has a plan too. • Built-in rest. Off-seasons, recovery, room for a second sport. They treat rest as part of development, not as falling behind — because the research is clear that the multi-sport, well-rested athletes are the ones who last and the ones who actually go further. • Radical transparency — about real all-in cost, about playing time, about expectations, about what your family is signing up for. • Coaches with actual training, and a program that invests in coach education. Given how little oversight exists in youth sports, a program that chooses to train its coaches is telling you what it values. • Honesty about outcomes. They'll talk about the athletes who left, got hurt, or stopped having fun — not just parade the few who "made it." Survivorship marketing is a fear-program tell; honest accounting is a development-program tell. • It's anchored in athlete-centered principles. The best programs now consciously align with something like the Aspen Institute's Children's Bill of Rights in Sports — the framework, endorsed by hundreds of organizations and a growing list of cities and states, that lays out the minimum conditions an athlete is owed in sport. A program that's heard of it and built around it is showing you its compass. • It wants athletes who want to be there. No scarcity pressure, because it's confident in what it offers.

How a development program measures success: are athletes staying, improving, and still in love with it? Trophies are a byproduct, not the scoreboard.

5. What a fear-based program sounds like You'll know it by what comes out of its mouth. A fear-based program sounds like urgency and scarcity, every time: • "If you don't commit now, you'll lose your spot." • "Everyone serious is playing year-round." • "This is the only path to the next level." • "Your athlete will fall behind if they take a season off." • "We don't really do multi-sport athletes here." • "It's the exposure here that gets athletes recruited." • "We're the top program — families would kill for this spot."

Hear the pattern? It's all pressure and no development. Every sentence is engineered to make you afraid of missing out, and not one of them describes how your athlete will actually get better. A development program recruits your athlete's growth. A fear program recruits your anxiety. Fear turns good parents into reactive parents — and fear-based programs are built to do exactly that to you, on purpose.

6. What should parents ask before joining a team, club, academy, or travel organization? Don't sign up off a highlight reel and a fee schedule. Sit down and ask — and watch how they answer as much as what they answer. Defensiveness to fair questions is its own answer.

The questions: 1. "What's your development philosophy, and what does a typical practice actually look like?" 2. "How is playing time decided — especially at the younger ages?" 3. "What's the real, all-in cost?" Fees, travel, lodging, gear, tournament entries, the hidden extras. The sticker price is never the price.

4. "What's the true time commitment?" Practices, travel, weekends, off-season expectations. 5. "Do you support multi-sport athletes, and is rest built in?" 6. "What are your coaches' backgrounds and training?" 7. "How do you communicate with families, and how do you handle concerns?" 8. "Can I watch a practice and talk to a few current families?" (And then talk to ones you pick, not just the testimonial parents they hand you.) 9. "What happens to an athlete who develops slower — do you keep developing them, or do they get sidelined?" 10. "What's your philosophy on injuries and overuse?" 11. (For 15-17): "How honest will you be with us about my athlete's realistic level and fit?"

This becomes your Program Evaluation Checklist at the end. The throughline: a good program welcomes these questions. A program that bristles just answered the most important one.

7. What to do when a program says, "If you don't play for us now, you won't have a spot later" First, name it for what it is: a sales tactic, not a fact. Scarcity plus urgency is the oldest pressure play in the book — car lots run on it, timeshares run on it, and now youth sports runs on it. The moment a program reaches for it, they've told you something important about themselves.

Three truths to hold onto when you hear it:

The development truth: almost no athlete's future is actually decided by one program at one age. The door they're telling you is closing isn't really closing. There are other teams, other seasons, other paths, and late bloomers blow past early committers all the time. The "only chance" is nearly always manufactured.

The relationship truth: a program that recruits with fear will coach with fear. The tactic isn't separate from the experience — it is the experience, a preview. They just showed you, for free, exactly who they'll be once they have your athlete and your money.

The self-respect truth: a spot that only exists because you're scared isn't a spot worth having. A program that genuinely wants your athlete because

your athlete belongs there will still want them next week, after you've had time to think.

So here's what you do: slow down on purpose. Use a line like — "We don't make decisions under that kind of deadline. If the only reason to say yes is fear of losing the spot, that's not a good enough reason for our family." Then watch what happens. A good program respects it. A fear program escalates — and that escalation is your answer. Walk. You didn't lose a spot. You dodged a culture.

The line for the parent: Never let a countdown clock raise your child. Decide from wisdom, not from the fear someone manufactured to sell you.

Choices and Voices

There are two things parents must evaluate early and often: the choices they make and the voices they allow into the athlete's world.

A choice may look like a team, a trainer, a tournament, a lesson, a showcase, an academy, a social media platform, or an evaluation. A voice may look like a coach, instructor, influencer, recruiter, travel director, ranking service, online guru, or another parent in a group chat.

Both matter.

Some voices create clarity. Some create urgency. Some make the athlete more confident. Some make the athlete more dependent. Some help the family unplug from fear. Some plug the family deeper into it.

Before you ask, "Is this opportunity good?" ask, "Is this voice trustworthy?"

A trusted voice understands age and stage. A trusted voice talks about school, health, sleep, recovery, confidence, and the family, not just performance. A trusted voice can explain development without making your athlete feel broken. A trusted voice does not need to make you afraid to make you listen.

A fear-based voice does the opposite. It tells you the train is leaving. It promises a shortcut. It sells one method as if every body should move the

same way. It makes your athlete dependent on the next paid answer. It creates robots instead of athletes who can think, adjust, and own the work.

The wrong advisor does not have to touch your athlete to damage the journey. They only have to get inside the parent's decision-making.

So guard the voices.

Your athlete's confidence, body, mindset, and future are too important to hand to the loudest adult in the room.

Chapter Tool

Coach Green Flags vs. Red Flags

Trust-Worthy Coach	Walk-Away Coach
Athletes leave tired but lit up.	Athletes leave smaller, quieter, afraid.
Demanding and warm.	"Tough" means shame and humiliation.
Teaches the why.	Demands obedience without reasons.
Develops the whole roster.	Uses the roster to serve the logo.
Honest without overselling.	Promises scholarships, rankings, and exposure.
Consistent win or lose.	Mood swings control the environment.
Welcomes fair questions.	Treats questions as betrayal.

Manages rest and injuries.

Pushes hurt athletes to keep the schedule.

The Program Evaluation Checklist Ask before you join. Watch how they answer, not just what they say.

- [ ] Can they clearly explain their development philosophy?

- [ ] Is playing time decided fairly, especially when athletes are young?

- [ ] Do I know the real all-in cost (fees + travel + gear + tournaments + extras)?

- [ ] Do I know the true time commitment, including off-season?

- [ ] Do they support multi-sport athletes and build in rest?

- [ ] Are the coaches trained, and does the program invest in them?

- [ ] Is communication clear, and are concerns handled well?

- [ ] Can I watch a practice and talk to families I choose?

- [ ] Do they keep developing the slower-developing athlete?

- [ ] Do they have a sane injury / overuse philosophy?

- [ ] (Ages 15-17) Will they be honest about my athlete's real level and fit? A good program welcomes every one of these. Bristling at fair questions is the answer.

The Scarcity-Pressure Response Script For "play now or lose your spot" — and every variation of it.

Recognize it: Urgency + scarcity = a sales tactic, not a fact.

Say it: > "We don't make decisions under that kind of deadline. If the only reason to say yes is fear of losing the spot, that's not a good enough reason for our family. We'll think it over and follow up."

Then watch: - Respects it -> maybe a real program. - Escalates the pressure -> that's your answer. Walk. A program that wants your athlete because they belong there will still want them next week. A spot that only exists when you're scared was never a spot worth having.

Chapter 22: Read the Room Before You Sign the Check

How to Evaluate Teams, Clubs, Academies, and Travel Programs

Before you hand a stranger your child and your money, you are allowed to evaluate them as carefully as they are evaluating your checkbook.

That sentence should be obvious, but it isn't, because the modern youth sports machine has flipped the relationship. Programs audition families now. They make you feel lucky to be considered, hint that spots are scarce, and

create just enough urgency that you sign before you've actually looked. And most parents go along with it, because the fear of missing the spot drowns out the quieter, smarter instinct that says: wait — who are these people, and is this actually good for my athlete?

I want to give you permission to be that quieter instinct's biggest ally. You are not being difficult by asking hard questions before you join a team, club, academy, or travel organization. You are being a parent. A good program will respect it. A program that bristles at it just answered your most important question for free.

Read the room, not the brochure

Every program has a brochure version of itself — the website, the logos on the wall, the highlight reel of the few who "made it," the confident pitch. None of that tells you what your athlete's Tuesday will actually feel like. To know that, you have to read the room, not the brochure.

Here's a trick I learned evaluating programs from the inside for decades, and it's the single most useful thing in this chapter: watch how the adults behave when nobody's being recruited. Go watch an ordinary practice — not a showcase, not a tournament, a regular Tuesday. Watch how the coaches talk to the athletes who aren't the stars. Watch the athlete on the end of the bench. Watch whether athletes leave practice tired but lifted, or quiet and smaller. Watch how the coach handles a mistake. The program's true character is on display every single practice; most parents just never go look at it.

I tell recruiting families the same thing about evaluating a college coach: watch how he treats his current players when no one is recruiting, watch how he talks about the players who left, watch how his current parents describe him. The fit is already on display. You just have to look at it honestly instead of looking at the trophy case.

The questions that cut through the pitch

When you sit down with a program, don't ask the questions that get rehearsed answers ("Are you a good program?"). Ask the ones that reveal how they actually operate, and pay as much attention to how they answer as to what they say:

What is your development philosophy, and what does an ordinary practice actually look like? (Listen for a real answer about how athletes get better — not a pitch about showcases and connections.)

How is playing time decided, especially at the younger ages? (Watch whether it's about development or about winning U12 banners on the backs of the early-matured athletes.)

What is the real, all-in cost — fees, travel, lodging, gear, tournament entries, the extras nobody mentions until you're in? (The sticker price is never the price.)

What's the true time commitment, including the off-season? Do you support multi-sport athletes and build in rest? What are your coaches' actual backgrounds and training? How do you communicate with families and handle concerns? Can I watch a practice and talk to a few current families I choose myself — not just the three you'd hand me?

And the one that reveals the most: what happens to an athlete who develops slowly? Do you keep developing them, or do they quietly stop getting reps? The answer to that question tells you whether they see your child as an athlete to build or a customer to retain.

The biggest mistake isn't doing too little

Here's something I've said to families for years, and it applies directly to choosing programs: the biggest mistake parents make isn't doing too little. It's doing too much. The families who try to be part of every program, every team, every academy at once usually produce a tired athlete and an empty bank account.

So when you evaluate a program, you're not just asking "is this good?" You're asking "is this the right thing, and what would it cost us to say yes — not just in money, but in the weekends, the rest, the second sport, the family rhythm we'd have to give up?" A great program that consumes a childhood your athlete wasn't ready to hand over is not a great fit. Less, chosen well, beats more, chosen out of fear, every single time.

Sign with your eyes open

You will feel pressure to decide quickly. Resist it. Real development is a years-long process; almost no good decision in it has to be made tonight. Go watch the practice. Ask the hard questions. Call the families you chose. Add up the true cost. And then decide from what you actually saw, not from the pitch you were given.

The check you're about to sign isn't just money. It's your athlete's time, body, and joy, and your family's rhythm. Read the room before you sign it.

Evaluate the Voice Behind the Offer The program is not the only thing you are evaluating. You are also evaluating the voice behind the pitch.

What are they selling? Do they profit if you say yes? Do they talk more about your athlete's development or your fear of missing out? Do they respect your family boundaries? Do they understand your athlete's current age and stage?

A quality voice should slow the room down. It should help you ask better questions. It should give your athlete a clearer path.

A sales voice often does the opposite. It speeds the room up. It makes you feel late. It makes you feel that every other family knows something you do not.

Read the room.

Then read the voice.

Chapter Tool

(See full tool in the Parent Toolkit Appendix.)

Chapter 23: Safe, Transparent, and Accountable

The Safeguarding Layer Every Parent Should Ask About

There is one category of question in youth sports that matters more than development, more than playing time, more than exposure, more than any of it — and it's the category parents are most afraid to ask about, because it feels awkward, distrustful, even paranoid.

It is not paranoid. It is the most basic duty you have. Before a program develops your child, it has to keep your child safe. And in an industry with almost no licensing, no universal oversight, and no guaranteed standards, the only person reliably checking whether the safeguarding is in place is you.

So let me take the awkwardness off it: asking a program about safety, supervision, and accountability is not an accusation. It's the same as asking

whether a daycare does background checks or whether a surgeon is board-certified. A good program expects these questions and has clear answers ready, because they've thought about it long before you walked in. The discomfort you feel asking is nothing compared to the discomfort of wishing you had.

Why this layer exists

Youth sports puts adults in positions of enormous power and trust over children — often alone, often traveling, often in locker rooms and hotels, often with the kind of authority an athlete won't question. The overwhelming majority of coaches and staff are exactly who they appear to be: caring adults who'd protect your athlete with their lives. But the structure that lets the good ones do good is the same structure that, without safeguards, can be exploited by the rare bad one. Safeguarding isn't about assuming the worst of people. It's about building a system where the worst can't easily happen, regardless of who's in the room.

That system has a name in the best organizations — safeguarding — and it's made of specific, askable things.

What to actually ask about

A program that takes safety seriously will be able to answer all of these without defensiveness:

Do you run background checks on coaches and staff, and how often? What are your supervision policies — are athletes ever alone with a single adult? What are your rules around one-on-one communication with minors, including texting, social media, and private messaging? Are parents allowed to observe practices and be present, or are they kept at a distance? (Programs that discourage parents from watching deserve a hard second look.)

Then the medical and emergency layer, which parents forget because it's not dramatic until the day it is: Is there an emergency action plan? A heat and hydration plan for hot-weather training? A concussion protocol — who decides when an athlete sits and when they return? An injury reporting process and a clear medical decision process? Who's making the call when your athlete gets hurt and you're not there?

And the accountability layer: Is there a clear process for reporting a concern — and is it safe to use, or does raising a concern get a family quietly punished? What are the overnight travel expectations, the transportation rules, the boundaries around locker rooms, hotels, and facilities?

None of these questions is rude. Every one of them is a normal part of entrusting your child to an organization, and the asking itself signals to a program that your family is paying attention — which, frankly, makes your athlete safer.

Transparency is the tell

You don't need to become an investigator. In practice, the single best indicator is transparency. Safe, accountable programs are transparent by default — they tell you the policies before you ask, they welcome parents, they explain how decisions get made, they have nothing to hide because they built the thing to be seen. Programs that are vague, that discourage observation, that get irritated by safety questions, that have no clear answer for "who decides when my concussed athlete plays again" — that vagueness is the warning.

A program's willingness to be seen is the clearest sign it's safe to be in.

The non-negotiable

Everything else in this book — development, joy, the long game, the 40-year plan — assumes a child who is safe. That assumption is the floor under all of it, and you do not negotiate the floor. No amount of elite coaching, exposure, or winning is worth a program that can't or won't keep your child safe and accountable.

So before you're dazzled by the facility, the record, or the pitch, ask the boring, awkward, essential questions. A program that answers them gladly has earned a real look. A program that won't has told you everything you need to know.

Chapter Tool

(See full tool in the Parent Toolkit Appendix.)

Chapter 24: The Comparison Machine

Social Media, Rankings, Highlights, and the Athlete's Identity

Here's the shift, in one sentence: social media turned development into performance. Development is private, slow, boring, and invisible — a athlete getting a little better in an empty gym on a Tuesday. Performance is public, instant, measured, and addictive — a clip, a like, a ranking, a repost. We took the quiet thing that actually makes athletes and buried it under the loud thing that just makes content. And then we wondered why our athletes got anxious.

This isn't a "phones are bad, get off my lawn" chapter. Technology has genuine uses — film study, communication, even legitimate recruiting exposure for the right athlete at the right time. The danger isn't the tool. The danger is what the tool quietly does to an athlete's sense of who they are and whether they're enough. That's the whole chapter: protecting the athlete's identity from the machine.

1. How has social media changed youth sports? It rewired the whole thing in four ways.

It made everything public. A bad game used to live in a gym and die there. Now it can be filmed, posted, and compared. An athlete performs knowing the lens is always on — and performing for a lens is different from playing for the love of it.

It made everything comparable, all the time. Your athlete no longer measures against the dozen athletes in their gym. They measure against thousands of curated highlight reels from everywhere, each one engineered to look effortless. It's a comparison faucet that never shuts off.

It turned parents into publicists and athletes into brands. Especially now that NIL has trickled all the way down to high school and even grassroots — there's real pressure to "build a brand early," rack up followers, get on the ranking platforms. A twelve-year-old does not need a brand. A twelve-year- old needs a jump shot and a bedtime.

It moved the scoreboard inside the athlete's head and made it permanent. The old scoreboard reset every game. The new one — likes, follows, rankings, who reposted you — runs 24 hours a day and follows them to bed.

And the cost is showing up in the data. The Surgeon General has warned that teens who use social media heavily carry roughly double the risk of depression and anxiety symptoms, with compulsive use wrecking sleep and attention. The response has gone mainstream fast: by 2026, the majority of states have moved to regulate athletes' social media or ban phones in schools, and some countries have barred younger teens outright. Now — honest caveat, because this book doesn't traffic in panic — a lot of that research is correlational, and serious people debate how much is cause versus correlation.

But you don't need a settled meta-analysis to coach your own athlete. You can watch what the phone does to them, on their face, after their game. Trust that data. It's the only sample size that matters in your house.

When Your Athlete Becomes Content

Modern youth sports does not only ask athletes to compete.

It asks them to be filmed, streamed, clipped, tagged, ranked, reposted, and packaged.

Before parents chase visibility, they need to understand what visibility costs. It can cost privacy. It can cost control. It can cost quiet development. It can turn a child into content before that child has the maturity to understand what is being captured, shared, stored, and judged.

This does not mean all video is bad. Film can teach. Video can help recruiting. Streaming can let grandparents watch. Technology can be useful.

But useful tools become dangerous when families stop asking who owns the footage, who profits from the platform, who is watching, what rights are being granted, and what pressure the athlete feels knowing every mistake might be visible.

The question is not simply, "Can my athlete be seen?"

The better question

is, "What is being taken from my athlete when they are always visible?"
A young athlete needs space to grow off camera.

The work in the dark is still the real thing.

2. What do rankings do to parents emotionally? They hijack you. Rankings are built — quite literally, as a business — to generate the exact emotion that keeps you clicking: anxiety. A number next to your athlete's name, a number next to the athlete across town, and suddenly you're not a parent watching your child grow, you're a shareholder

watching a stock. Up: euphoria, validation, "we're on track." Down or absent: panic, comparison, "what are we missing." Neither feeling has anything to do with your athlete's actual development. Both feelings get you refreshing the page.

And here's what parents miss: the ranking services run on engagement. Drama, movement, hot takes, debate — that's the product. Your emotional investment isn't a side effect; it's the business model. The calmest, healthiest thing a parent can do is treat rankings the way you'd treat a horoscope: occasionally amusing, never a basis for a decision, and absolutely not a measure of your child's worth or your worth as a parent.

3. What do rankings do to athletes mentally? They quietly swap the athlete's question. A developing athlete should be asking "Am I getting better?" — a

question they can answer with work, every day, in their control. Rankings replace it with "Where do I rank?" — a question they can't control, that depends on other athletes, on subjective evaluators, on who paid for what exposure, on pure noise. You've taken an athlete with an internal compass and handed them an external one that spins.

The mental damage compounds: a ranked athlete can start playing not to fall instead of playing to grow — protecting a number instead of taking the risks that actually develop them. An unranked or low-ranked athlete can decide the verdict is in and quit trying. Either way, the ranking became the identity, and a ranking is a snapshot sold as a verdict — a single frame of a moving picture, often wrong, always temporary. The most dangerous sentence a young athlete can absorb is "I am a three-star," because now a number gets to tell them who they are. Late bloomers blow past early rankings constantly. The feed is noise; what your athlete builds in the dark is the signal. Teach them to trust that signal.

4. When does posting highlights become pressure? The moment the posting starts driving the playing. There's a clean line here: • Healthy: the athlete does the work, has a good game, and a clip happens to capture it. The post is a byproduct of the performance. • Pressure: the athlete starts playing for the clip — forcing the flashy play, checking who saw it, measuring the game by the footage instead of the work, deflating if a good performance didn't get filmed or didn't get likes. Now the performance is a byproduct of the post, and the tail is wagging the dog.

Other tells it's tipped into pressure: anxiety when a post underperforms, comparing their clips' numbers to teammates', editing reality to look better than the game was, or a parent who's clearly more invested in the highlight than the athlete is. When the highlight reel starts editing the athlete — changing how they play to feed the feed — it's no longer a tool. It's the boss.

5. Should young athletes have sports-specific social media pages? Depends entirely on age and purpose, and the test is one question: is this a tool for the work, or a stage for the self?

For younger athletes (roughly under 15): generally no. There's no real recruiting reason — college coaches aren't scouting twelve-year-olds off Instagram — so the only thing a sports page does at that age is plug the athlete into the comparison-and-metrics machine years before they need to be there. All risk, no payoff. If the family wants to keep a highlight archive, keep it private — a folder, not a feed.

For older athletes (15-17) actively recruiting: it can be a legitimate tool, with guardrails. A clean, professional highlight account used to share film with coaches has a real purpose. But it works only if: an adult co-manages it, it's treated as a professional portfolio and not a popularity contest, follower counts and likes are explicitly not the point, and the athlete's identity is anchored somewhere it can't be touched by a comment section. The instant the page becomes about validation instead of recruiting, it's stopped being a tool and started being a hook. Purpose decides. A recruiting tool serves the athlete. A validation stage consumes them.

6. What should parents avoid posting? Parents do real damage here without meaning to, because they're proud and the platform rewards it. Avoid: • Anything that turns your athlete into your highlight reel. If your feed is a running stat line of their performance, you've made their athletic output your content, and they feel it. • Comparisons and rankings. Posting where they placed, who they "beat," their ranking — it teaches them that's what matters to you. • Their failures, struggles, or your disappointment. Ever. Their bad games are not your content.

• Tagging coaches, programs, or recruiters to pressure or campaign. It embarrasses the athlete and annoys the adults. • Their location, schedule, school, and routine in real time. That's a safety issue, full stop — you're broadcasting where a minor will be and when. • Stat-and-offer updates that read as a résumé. It makes a childhood look like a job search and puts your anxiety on public display.

The gut check before any post: Am I posting this for my athlete, or for me? If it's for you — the validation, the pride, the "look at us" — keep it in the camera roll.

7. What should athletes avoid posting? Worth teaching directly, because it protects both their head and their future: • Anything that ties their mood to the metrics — posting for the likes, then living and dying by the count. • Trash talk, drama, and clapbacks. Coaches and recruiters absolutely look, and character shows. One bad post can cost a real opportunity. • Anything they'd be embarrassed for a coach, a college, or a future employer to see. The internet is a permanent record with no delete key that actually works. • Their lowest moments and rawest emotions in real time. Post- loss is the worst time to post anything. • Beefing with refs, coaches, teammates, or opponents. It tells every program watching exactly what they'd be signing up for. • Oversharing location and routine — same safety issue as for parents.

The frame for the athlete: the internet is a job interview that never ends, and the people who decide your future are watching the version of you that you choose to show. Show the worker, not the whiner.

8. How do likes, reposts, rankings, and highlight clips distort identity? They move the athlete's sense of self outside their own body and into a feed they don't control. A healthy athletic identity is built from the inside: I work hard, I'm getting better, I love this, I know who I am. The metrics offer a

counterfeit version built from the outside: I am as good as my last clip's numbers, I am my ranking, I am how many people reposted me. The counterfeit feels great when the numbers are up — and collapses the instant they're down, or worse, silent.

That's the cruelest part: the engine doesn't just punish bad numbers, it punishes silence. An athlete can have a great game, post it, and get crickets — and conclude they're nothing, because the machine taught them that unwitnessed effort doesn't count. That's a catastrophe for an athlete, because almost all real development is unwitnessed. The thousand reps nobody filmed are the whole game. An athlete whose identity lives in the feed will abandon the unglamorous work that actually builds them, because it doesn't generate content. They'll chase the clip and starve the craft. Identity built on attention is identity built on sand — and puberty, slumps, injuries, and silence are the tide.

9. How should parents talk about online comparison? Not by banning and lecturing — that just makes the phone forbidden fruit and ends the conversation. Talk about the machinery, repeatedly and without judgment, until the athlete can see it running themselves. The core message, said a hundred different ways:

"That's a highlight, not a life. You're comparing your behind-the-scenes — every missed shot, every bad practice, every awkward growth-spurt week — to someone's edited trailer. Nobody posts the airball. You're losing a contest that was rigged before you opened the app."

Then add the part that actually builds armor: redirect them from comparison back to their own path and their own work. "Forget where they are. Are you better than you were last month? That's the only scoreboard that's real." And model it — a parent who openly compares their own life, body, or athlete to others online is teaching the comparison habit louder than any talk can undo. Name the rigged game out loud, point them back to their own lane, and show them you're not playing the comparison game either.

10. What is the difference between using social media responsibly and building a child's identity around attention? It's the difference between an athlete who has an account and an athlete the account has.

Responsible use: the phone is a tool the athlete picks up for a reason and puts down. Their worth, their mood, and their motivation come from off-line sources — the work, the relationships, the love of the game, the family. They could lose every follower tomorrow and still know exactly who they are. Social media is in their life; it isn't their life.

Identity built on attention: the metrics are the mood. Likes set the self-esteem, silence triggers a crisis, the ranking defines the worth, the next post is always pulling at them. The athlete isn't using the platform — the platform is using the athlete, and it's wired straight into their sense of self. A slump isn't a slump anymore; it's an identity collapse, because there's no self underneath the stats to fall back on.

The gut check, for the athlete and the parent both: If the phone disappeared for a month, who would your athlete be? If the answer is "an athlete who works, a person with people who love them, an athlete who loves the game" — you're fine, the tool is a tool. If the honest answer is "lost, anxious, like they don't exist" — the engine has the wheel, and your job is to take it back. Not by smashing the phone. By rebuilding, loudly and daily, the off-line identity the machine has been quietly eroding: You are not your numbers. You never were.

The work in the dark is the real thing, and I'd love you exactly the same if not one person ever watched.

Chapter Tool

The Post / Don't Post Guide

For Parents

Fine to post
Keep in the camera roll
Occasional joy and team/community moments.
A running stat line of performance.
Milestones the athlete is proud of.
Rankings, placements, and "who we beat."
Private archived film for recruiting.
Failures, struggles, or your disappointment.
Gratitude and perspective.
Real-time location, schedule, school, or routine.
General season memories.
Tagging coaches or recruiters to campaign.
Gut check: Am I posting this for my athlete, or for me?

For Athletes

Show this
Never post this
The work, the worker, and good teammate moments.
Trash talk, clapbacks, and arguing with officials or coaches.
Clips that happened to capture good play.
Clips you forced the game to create.
Gratitude, growth, and the grind.
Raw emotion right after a loss.
A clean recruiting highlight, when age-appropriate and adult-managed.
Anything a college or employer should not see.
Frame: the internet is a job interview that never ends. Show the worker, not the whiner.

|| A clean recruiting highlight (15-17, adult-managed) | Anything a college or employer shouldn't see | Frame: the internet is a job interview that never ends. Show the worker, not the whiner.

The Rankings Reality Card

• A ranking is a snapshot sold as a verdict — one frame of a moving picture, often wrong, always temporary.

• Ranking services run on engagement; your anxiety is the business model, not a side effect.

• The real question is "Am I getting better?" (in your control) — not "Where do I rank?" (noise).

• Late bloomers pass early rankings constantly. What the algorithm shows is noise; what your athlete builds in the dark is signal.

• Treat rankings like a horoscope: occasionally amusing, never a decision, never a measure of worth.

The Identity Gut-Check If the phone disappeared for a month, who would your athlete be? — "An athlete who works, a person who's loved, an athlete who loves the game" -> the tool is a tool. You're fine. — "Lost, anxious, like they don't exist" -> the engine has the wheel. Take it back — not by smashing the phone, but by rebuilding the off-line identity daily: You are not your numbers.

The work in the dark is the real thing. I'd love you the same if no one ever watched.

Chapter 25: Rankings Are Not a Verdict

Why the Board Is Noise and the Work Is Signal

A ranking is not an identity. It is not a future. It is not a measure of a parent's worth. It is a snapshot sold as a verdict.

Hold onto that last line, because it explains almost everything painful that rankings do to families. A ranking takes a single moment — one evaluator's opinion, on one day, of where an athlete happens to be in a process that is nowhere near finished — and dresses it up as a final judgment. And once something looks like a verdict, parents and athletes start treating it like destiny. They refresh it. They internalize it. They make real decisions from it. They let a number assign worth.

I've sat on the side of the desk where these judgments get made, and I want to tell you plainly what a youth ranking actually is and isn't, because the truth is far more freeing than the fear.

What a ranking actually measures

Rankings feel objective because they come as numbers. They are not. A youth ranking is influenced by a long list of things that have little to do with how good an athlete will eventually be: access (who got seen by the right people), visibility (who plays for the program that gets covered), event participation (who could afford the circuit), timing (who was hot the week the evaluator watched), maturity (who hit puberty first), geography (who's in a hotbed versus a quiet corner), and pure subjective opinion (what that particular evaluator happens to value).

Stack all that up and you get a number that says far more about an athlete's circumstances and stage than about their ceiling. The early bloomer sits high because his body arrived first. The late bloomer doesn't appear at all because his hasn't — yet. Neither number is a measurement of the athlete they'll become. They're a measurement of the morning the photo was taken.

A late bloomer may not show up on a board at fourteen and pass half that board by seventeen. An early bloomer may sit near the top before the field catches up and quietly slides off. I have watched both happen more times than I can count. The board is a weather report, and the weather changes.

What rankings do to the mind

The real damage isn't the number. It's what the number does to the question an athlete is asking themselves.

A developing athlete should be asking: Am I getting better? That question is gold, because it points at things inside the athlete's control — the work, the habits, the reps, the recovery, the coachability, the daily choices. It's a question they can answer with effort, every single day.

A ranking swaps it for a different question: Where do I rank? And that question is poison, because the answer is entirely outside the athlete's control. It depends on other athletes, on evaluators, on access, on noise. An athlete who lives by "where do I rank" hands the steering wheel of their self- worth to a machine that profits from their anxiety — because, make no mistake, the ranking services run on engagement, and a calm, unbothered family is bad for their business.

So the athlete who's ranked starts playing not to fall instead of playing to grow. And the athlete who's unranked or ranked low decides the verdict is in and stops trying. Both have let a snapshot become a self-image.

Return the question

The job of a parent here is simple and powerful: keep returning your athlete to the only question that builds anything. Not "where do you rank?" but "are you getting better?" Point them at the work, the habits, the body, the mind, the classroom, the coachability, the daily choices — all the things the board can't see and the athlete can actually control.

Treat the rankings the way you'd treat a horoscope. Occasionally interesting. Mildly entertaining. Absolutely never a basis for a decision, and never, ever a measure of your child's worth or your worth as a parent. When the board ticks up, enjoy it for a second and let it go. When it ticks down or never mentions your athlete, shrug and get back to work.

The board is noise. The work is signal. Teach your athlete to tune out the noise and trust the signal, and you will have given them something far more valuable than any ranking: an internal compass that points at the work, no matter what the number says.

Chapter Tool

(See full tool in the Parent Toolkit Appendix.)

Chapter 26: Exposure or Exposed?

Showcases, Camps, Tournaments, Rankings, and the Myth of Being Seen

Showcases, Camps, Tournaments, Rankings, and the Myth of Being Seen Start with the title, because it's the entire chapter. There are two things that can happen when you put your athlete in front of evaluators:

Exposure — a ready athlete gets seen by the right people at the right time, and doors open.

Exposed — an athlete who isn't ready yet gets put on display, and the right people see exactly that. Or worse — there are no "right people" there at all, and you just paid for a weekend of being watched by nobody who matters while your athlete's body and the family's bank account took the hit.

The marketing sells you the first word. Most of what's for sale delivers the second. Knowing the difference is worth more than any showcase you'll ever buy.

And the economics make it urgent. Families now spend an average of over a thousand dollars a year on a single sport — up nearly half in just a few years — and a huge slice of that goes to exposure: showcases, combines, ranking events, travel tournaments, camps. Meanwhile the college funnel actually got narrower recently — the House settlement's roster caps compressed rosters and erased thousands of spots, hitting the developmental "give-him- a-chance" recruit hardest. So the exposure economy is charging more for entry to a building with fewer doors. That's not a reason to panic. It's a reason to be ruthless about which events are real.

1. When is a showcase, camp, combine, tournament, or exposure event actually useful? When three things line up: the athlete is ready, the right evaluators are actually there, and the timing is right in the recruiting calendar. Miss any one and you've bought exposure that exposes nothing.

The genuinely useful cases:

• A rising junior or senior who's already producing, has current film and a player profile ready, attends an NCAA-certified event during a live evaluation period where coaches from realistic-fit programs will actually be present. That's real exposure. That's the machine working as advertised. • A college's own camp at a school the athlete has genuine interest in and realistic fit for — because the people evaluating are the exact people who could offer. • A development camp sold honestly as development — great coaching, great reps, a chance to compete up — where nobody pretended scouts would be watching. Useful for the work, not the recruiting. Just know which one you bought. • A tournament that's part of the season's natural rhythm and good competition, not an extra "can't-miss" bolt-on draining the calendar.

The test: useful events have a clear, honest purpose you can name — this develops my athlete or this gets my ready athlete in front of these specific coaches at the right time. "Exposure" with no name attached is a vibe with an invoice.

2. When is it too early? Most of the time it's sold, honestly. It's too early when: • The athlete isn't at recruiting age yet. College coaches are not building their classes off twelve-year-olds, and they can't evaluate them off-campus anyway. A "national exposure showcase" for fifth graders is selling parents a feeling, not a future. • The athlete isn't ready to be evaluated (see the next question) — meaning being seen now just gets them seen not being ready. • There's no film, no profile, no plan — the athlete isn't equipped to convert exposure into anything even if it happened. • It's during a dead period or it isn't certified — meaning, by rule, no college coach can be there evaluating, no matter what the event promises. • The family is doing it from fear — "everyone's going" — rather than from a real recruiting need.

The rule of thumb: before an athlete is a rising junior with something to show, almost every "exposure" event is really a development event or a revenue

event wearing an exposure costume. Pay for development if it's good development. Don't pay exposure prices for it.

3. What does "ready to be evaluated" mean across sports? It means the athlete is far enough along that being seen helps instead of hurts. The specifics vary by sport, but the principle is universal: an evaluator should walk away thinking "I want to keep watching this athlete," not "this athlete isn't there yet." You only get so many first impressions with the same coaches.

What "ready" looks like, across sports: • The fundamentals are solid and reliable under game speed and pressure — not just on a good day. • The athlete can compete at the level of the event without being overwhelmed. Being the weakest athlete in the gym in front of scouts is the definition of exposed. • The body is developed enough to show what the athlete actually is — not mid-growth-spurt and temporarily clumsy (a snapshot taken during the awkward phase undersells an athlete badly). • There's a real "thing" — a position, a tool, a translatable skill an evaluator can project forward. • The athlete handles the moment emotionally — nerves don't erase the ability.

"Ready" is rarely about a birthday. It's about whether your athlete showing up there advances them or labels them. If you're not sure they're ready, they probably aren't — and waited-and-ready beats early-and-exposed every time.

4. What are parents really buying emotionally when they pay for exposure? Relief. That's the honest product. Underneath the entry fee, parents are buying: • Relief from the fear of falling behind — the sense that doing something means we're not neglecting the dream. • The feeling of being a good, proactive parent — "we're giving them every opportunity."

• Hope, packaged and sold — a ticket that says maybe this is the one where someone discovers them. • An answer to the group chat — so when everyone asks "are you going to the thing," you can say yes and not feel like the parent who's slacking.

None of that is about the athlete's development. It's about soothing the parent's anxiety — and the exposure industry knows it, which is exactly why the marketing targets your fear and not your athlete's skill set. There's nothing shameful about the fear; every parent feels it. But you have to be able to see clearly that the fear is the thing being monetized. When you catch yourself reaching for the credit card to feel better, pause — that's a fear purchase, and fear is a terrible financial advisor.

5. What questions should parents ask before paying? Run every exposure event through this, on top of the basic before-you-pay filter from earlier in the book: 1. "Is my athlete actually ready to be evaluated?" (If no, it's development at best, exposure never.) 2. "Is my athlete at a recruiting stage where this matters?" (Rising junior/senior with film, or not.) 3. "Is this event NCAA-certified, and does it fall in a live evaluation period for our sport?" (If not, coaches cannot be there evaluating — by rule.) 4. "Which specific programs and coaches will actually attend — and can I verify it, not just take the flyer's word?" 5. "Is this realistic fit exposure?" (A showcase full of coaches from programs your athlete will never play for is tourism.) 6. "What's the real all-in cost — fee, travel, lodging, time, missed rest — and what's the honest expected value?" 7. "Am I doing this from a plan, or from fear that everyone else is going?"

The throughline from the whole book: a good event welcomes these questions and answers them straight. An event that gets vague, defensive, or leans on urgency just answered the most important one.

6. How can parents tell if the right coaches, scouts, or evaluators will actually be present? This is where most families get fleeced, so here's the concrete, unglamorous truth: recruiting is governed by a calendar, and the calendar tells you whether evaluators can even be there.

College coaches can only evaluate athletes in person at NCAA-certified events during designated live (evaluation) periods. Outside those windows — during dead periods especially — they are flat-out prohibited from in- person evaluation; only digital contact is allowed. So: • Check the event against the NCAA recruiting calendar for your sport. (Every sport has its own; the dates shift yearly — find the official one.) If the event lands in a dead period, no college coach is legally there to evaluate, regardless of what the marketing implies. • Confirm the event is NCAA-certified if its whole pitch is college exposure. Uncertified "exposure showcase"? Coaches can't use it for evaluation. • Ask for the specific list of programs sending coaches — and verify independently. "College coaches will be in attendance" is the oldest line in the business. Which ones? From where? At your athlete's realistic level? A legitimate event names names. A fishy one stays vague. • Match it to your athlete's recruiting stage. The major live-period events (like the summer windows when most offers cluster) are built for rising juniors and seniors who are ready. A younger athlete at the same event is paying for a ticket to a show that isn't about them.

Bottom line: if an event can't tell you who is coming and can't legally have evaluators there given the calendar and certification, you are not buying exposure. You're buying a weekend.

7. What is the difference between a developmental event and a performative event? This distinction will save you thousands of dollars and a lot of your athlete's joy.

A developmental event exists to make your athlete better. Great coaching, hard reps, real competition, instruction, feedback. The athlete leaves improved. Success is measured in growth.

A performative event exists to make your athlete seen (or to make the organizer money off the promise of it). It's a stage, not a classroom. The athlete leaves the same as they arrived — maybe ranked, maybe filmed, maybe nothing — but no more skilled. Success is measured in attention.

Both can be legitimate if you know which one you bought and your athlete is at the right stage for it. The trouble starts when families pay performative prices and time for an event that delivers no development, while their athlete is years away from needing exposure — so they get neither growth nor real visibility, just an invoice and a tired athlete. The tell: a developmental event talks about what your athlete will learn. A performative event talks about who will see them. For most athletes most of the time, the developmental event is the better buy — because development is the thing that makes the exposure worth having later.

8. What should parents understand about highlight videos? That a highlight video is a door-opener, not a closer — and that it cuts both ways.

What it's good for: getting a coach to spend ninety seconds deciding whether to watch more. That's its entire job. A clean, current highlight reel with a few seconds of context and the best honest plays can earn an athlete a longer look. In the modern, film-and-database recruiting world, it's often the first contact a coach has with an athlete — more than the live showcase.

What parents misunderstand: • It opens the door; it doesn't get the offer. Coaches know highlights are the best 90 seconds of a career. They use them to decide whether to dig deeper — then they watch full game film, where the truth lives. • An oversold reel backfires. A highlight tape that's flashier than the player creates a gap between the clip and the athlete, and coaches who feel "sold" tune out. Honest is more effective than impressive. • Full game film matters more for serious evaluation. The reel gets the look; the unedited game gets the read. Make sure the real film exists and holds up.

• It does not need to be expensive or pro-produced. Coaches care about the player, not the production. A clean DIY reel with good clips beats a glossy one over a mediocre player.

And tie it back to the last chapter: a highlight reel is a recruiting tool, not a content product. The minute it's being made for likes instead of for coaches, it's left its lane.

9. What is the danger of chasing visibility before readiness? You spend the resource you can't get back — first impressions — on a version of your athlete that isn't the real one yet. Coaches talk, remember, and form impressions fast. Put an unready athlete in front of evaluators and the label that sticks isn't "promising" — it's "not there." Then when the athlete is ready a year later, they're fighting a first impression instead of making one.

The other dangers stack up: • You drain the resources — money, weekends, rest, the family calendar — that should've gone into the development that would've made the athlete actually ready. • You teach the athlete the wrong scoreboard — that being seen matters more than getting good, which is the exact identity poison from the social media chapter, just offline. • You risk the body and the joy chasing an event the athlete didn't need, often during a stretch they should've been resting.

The principle, one more time because it's the spine of this whole book: develop first, get seen second. You cannot expose your way to being good. You can get good and then get seen — and a ready athlete in front of the right people doesn't need to chase visibility, because readiness creates its own gravity. Build the athlete. Then let them be seen.

10. What would you say to the parent who believes one missed event could cost their athlete's future? I'd put a hand on their shoulder and say: that's the fear talking, and the fear is wrong. Almost no athlete's future has ever been decided by attending or missing one event. That's not how recruiting works, and it's never been how it works.

Here's the truth that defuses it: coaches recruit players who can play — and an athlete who can play gets found. Recruiting today runs on film, databases, relationships, and multiple touchpoints over time, not one magic afternoon where a scout discovers a hidden gem and everything changes. If your athlete is good and developing, missing one showcase doesn't end anything — there will be other events, other film, other windows, an entire recruiting calendar full of chances. And if your athlete isn't ready, that one event wasn't going to save them anyway; it was just going to expose them early.

The "one missed event ends it all" feeling is manufactured. It's the single most profitable lie in the exposure economy, because a parent who believes it will pay anything, anytime, out of pure terror of the closing door. But the door isn't closing. The talent gets found. The work gets seen. A ready athlete is not discovered at one event — they're revealed over time by the body of work. So miss the event if you need to. Rest the athlete. Protect the weekend. Keep building. The future is not being decided that Saturday — you're just being told it is, by someone selling tickets.

The line for the parent: The talent gets found. Your only job is to make sure there's talent to find — and an athlete who still loves it when they're found.

Visibility Without Readiness Being seen does not help if what coaches see is an athlete who is not yet ready.

That is the hard truth behind exposure.

Parents often believe visibility creates opportunity. Sometimes it does. But only when the athlete has enough readiness for the visibility to work in their favor. If the athlete lacks strength, skill, confidence, body language, coachability, academic habits, or emotional maturity, then the stage does not create opportunity. It reveals what is missing.

That is not always bad. Truth can help. But do not pay exposure prices when what your athlete needs is development.

Develop first.

Get seen second.

Chapter Tool

The "Is This Real Exposure?" Filter For any showcase, combine, ranking event, or "exposure" camp. All five should clear.

1. Ready? — Is my athlete actually ready to be evaluated, not just old enough?

2. Stage? — Rising junior/senior with current film and a profile? (If not, this is development or revenue, not exposure.)

3. Calendar + Certified? — Is it an NCAA-certified event in a live evaluation period for our sport? (If not, coaches cannot evaluate — by rule.)

4. Who, verified? — Can they name the specific programs/coaches attending, at my athlete's realistic level — and can I confirm it independently?

5. Honest value? — Real all-in cost vs. honest expected return — and am I doing this from a plan, not from fear? Vague answers, urgency, or "coaches will be there" with no names = you're buying a weekend, not exposure.

Developmental vs. Performative
Event

Developmental
Performative
Great coaching, hard reps, and real instruction.

A stage with little to no teaching.
Athlete leaves improved.
Athlete leaves the same, maybe filmed or ranked.
Success equals growth.
Success equals attention.
Talks about what the athlete will learn.
Talks about who will see the athlete.
Useful at many ages if done well.
Useful only when the athlete is ready and timing is right.

Both can be legitimate if you know which one you bought. Paying performative prices for a developmental need is where families lose money, time, and joy.

The Highlight Video Rules

• It's a door-opener, not a closer — its only job is to earn a longer look.

• Coaches decide in ~90 seconds whether to watch full game film, where the truth lives.

• Honest beats impressive — an oversold reel makes coaches tune out.

• Production doesn't matter; the player does. A clean DIY reel over a real player wins.

• It's a recruiting tool, not content. The moment it's for likes, it's left its lane.

The Fear-Purchase Gut-Check Before you pay for "exposure," ask: Am I buying my athlete an opportunity, or buying myself relief? — Opportunity -> ready athlete, real evaluators, right timing. Pay. — Relief -> "everyone's going," vague promises, a closing- door feeling. That's the fear being monetized. Sleep on it. The door isn't closing. The talent gets found.

Chapter 27: Developmental or Performative?

Knowing What You Are Actually Buying

One of the most expensive confusions in youth sports is the failure to know, before you pay, whether the thing you're buying exists to develop your athlete or to display them.

These are two completely different products. They cost similar money, use similar language, and often look alike from the outside. But they do opposite things, and families burn through thousands of dollars and dozens of weekends because they paid display prices for an athlete who needed development — or skipped real development chasing a display their athlete wasn't ready for.

Let me give you a clean way to tell them apart, because once you can, you'll never look at an event flyer the same way again.

The two products

A developmental event exists to help the athlete improve. It offers coaching, instruction, feedback, reps, challenge, and a clearer picture of what to work on. The athlete leaves better — or at least leaves knowing exactly what to go build. Success is measured in growth. A good skills camp, a well-run clinic, a development-focused team where your athlete actually plays and gets coached hard — these are developmental. They make the athlete more capable.

A performative event exists to put the athlete on a stage. Its product is visibility, attention, rankings, clips, or access. The athlete leaves the same as they arrived — maybe seen, maybe ranked, maybe filmed, but no more skilled. Success is measured in attention. A showcase, a combine, a ranking event, an exposure camp — these are performative. They display whatever the athlete already is.

Here's the crucial point: both can be legitimate. A performative event is genuinely valuable for the right athlete at the right time — a ready, recruiting-age athlete in front of the right evaluators. There's nothing wrong with the category. The problem is never the event. The problem is buying the wrong category for where your athlete actually is.

The tell

You can spot which one you're being sold in about thirty seconds, because they talk about completely different things.

The developmental event talks about what your athlete will learn. The instruction, the coaching, the reps, the feedback, the skill they'll build. Its pitch is about getting better.

The performative event talks about who will see them. The scouts, the rankings, the exposure, the clips, the "next level." Its pitch is about being seen.

Listen for the verb. Learn versus seen. Once you hear it, you'll know exactly which product is on the table — and you can decide whether it matches what your athlete needs right now.

Why development is usually the better buy

For most athletes, most of the time, the developmental event is the smarter purchase. And the reason is a piece of logic the exposure economy desperately doesn't want you to follow to its conclusion:

Development is what makes exposure worth having later.

Think it through. A ready athlete in the right setting can absolutely benefit from being seen — exposure converts their readiness into opportunity. But an unready athlete on a stage isn't getting exposure. They're getting exposed. Evaluators don't see promise; they see an athlete who isn't there yet, and that's the impression that sticks. You've spent display money to broadcast that your athlete isn't ready, while spending nothing on the development that would have made them ready.

So the order matters, and the culture has it backwards. Build first. Get seen second. The dollars you'd spend displaying an unready athlete are almost always better spent developing them — because a developed athlete creates their own exposure later, and an undeveloped one can't be exposed into being good.

Buy on purpose

Before you pay for any event, ask the one question that cuts through every flyer: Is this developing my athlete, or displaying my athlete — and which one does my athlete actually need right now?

If they need to get better, buy development, and don't let a showcase convince you it's the same thing. If they're genuinely ready to be seen, a performative event can be worth real money. Just know which one you bought, and buy it on purpose — not out of the fear that everyone else is going.

Listen for the verb. A developmental event tells you what your athlete will learn. A performative event tells you who will see them. Once you can hear which one is being sold, you stop buying the wrong one by accident — and you start buying on purpose.

Chapter Tool

(See full tool in the Parent Toolkit Appendix.)

Chapter 28: Highlight Videos and the Myth of One Big Moment

Recruiting Tool, Not Content

Somewhere in every recruiting-age family's journey comes the highlight video, and with it a quiet, expensive fantasy: that the right clip, edited the right way, posted at the right moment, could be the thing that changes everything. Let me take the pressure off that fantasy right now, because it sends families spending money and emotion in exactly the wrong place — and because I've sat on the other side of it, watching these reels come in, deciding in seconds which kids to keep looking at.

A highlight video is a useful, even necessary tool. But it is a door-opener, not a closer. Understanding that one distinction will save you from both overspending on it and overbelieving in it.

What the reel actually does — from the chair where it's watched

Here is the entire job of a highlight video: to get a coach to spend the next ninety seconds deciding whether to watch more. That's the whole job. In a recruiting world run on film and databases, the reel is often a coach's very first contact with an athlete — before the live look, before the email. A clean, current reel with a few seconds of context and the athlete's best honest plays earns a longer look.

But a longer look is all it earns. The reel opens the door; it does not get the offer. The actual evaluation happens in the full, unedited game film — the at-bats that didn't work, the defensive lapses, the body language between plays, the truth a highlight reel is designed to hide. Every coach knows a highlight reel is the best ninety seconds of a kid's career. They watch it to decide whether to go dig for the other ninety-nine percent.

The four mistakes — and the one that costs the most

I can tell you exactly how that looks from the chair where these reels get watched, because I've sat in it.

A friend in professional baseball once gave me the cleanest line I have ever heard for this. He said, "Why would I take a ten-year-old F-150 to a car show? There's nothing to show." He was talking about showcases, but the same rule applies to highlight videos. Parents want the car show before the truck has been built.

I have watched families rush to package an athlete before the athlete was ready to be evaluated. They add music, graphics, slow motion, hashtags, dramatic edits, and a polished introduction, but experienced coaches are not watching for production value. They are asking a much simpler question: is there something here worth a longer look? If the answer is no, the packaging does not help. In fact, it can hurt, because it tells the evaluator that the family may be more interested in selling the athlete than developing the athlete.

The best videos I have seen were often the simplest: clean angle, clear view, honest reps, no hiding, no pretending. A coach does not need a movie trailer. A coach needs evidence. Before you pay to show the athlete, make sure there is something developmentally ready to show.

That's what a highlight video can and can't do, seen from the other side of the desk.

Four mistakes show up over and over. Families think the reel closes the deal — it doesn't; it opens the door to the full film where the real evaluation lives. They oversell it — and this is the costly one: a reel flashier than the player creates a gap between the clip and the kid, and an experienced coach who feels "sold" doesn't just discount the reel, they trust the whole family less. Honest beats impressive every single time. Families forget the full film matters more — the reel gets the look, the unedited game gets the read, so the real film had better exist and hold up. And they spend like it's a movie — a clean phone-shot reel of good plays beats an expensive, over-produced package over a weaker player every time. Save that money for development, which is the only thing that actually changes the evaluation.

Keep the whole approach brutally simple: send video, a schedule, a transcript, and three honest sentences. That's what a coach needs to do their job. Make it easy and they'll do it. Pile on more and they stop reading.

The bigger myth underneath

Beneath the highlight-video fantasy is a larger one that runs through this whole part of the book: the belief that there's one big moment — one clip, one showcase, one game, one email — that makes or breaks a child's future. There almost never is. Recruiting runs on film, databases, relationships, and many touchpoints over time. Coaches don't discover a hidden gem in a single magic afternoon and change a life on the spot. They evaluate players who can play, repeatedly, from many angles. The kid who is good and developing gets found — not because of one perfect clip, but because the body of work holds up to a second, third, and fourth look.

So a highlight video is exactly what its name says: a tool to highlight an athlete who already has something worth highlighting. The moment a reel is being built for likes instead of for coaches, it has left its lane and become content — and content is a costume the recruiting world sees through instantly. Keep it a tool. Make it clean, honest, and current. Point it at the right people. And then stop believing it's the one big moment, because the only thing that was ever going to get your child recruited is the thing the reel can only point at: a real player, doing real things, that holds up when a coach goes looking for the truth. Build that. The reel is just the knock on the door.

Chapter Tool

The Highlight Video Reality Check

Before you spend a dollar or lose a night of sleep over a reel, ask: Is this clean, current, and watchable in the first ten seconds? Does it show honest best plays, not manufactured ones? Does the real, unedited game film exist and hold up to it? Am I building this for coaches, or for likes? And the gut-check: am I spending on the reel because it's easier than investing in the player — easier to edit a video than to do the slow work that's the only thing the video could ever point to?

A reel opens a door. Only a real player walks through it.

Part VI — The Parent's Role

Chapter 29: The Car Ride Home

The Most Important Fifteen Minutes You Will Ever Get Wrong

If I could reach into your family and change one single thing — one habit, across every sport, every level, every family in America — I wouldn't touch the training, the team, or the money.

I'd fix the drive home.

Because I've asked thousands of grown athletes what they actually remember from all those years, and almost none of them lead with a game. They don't remember the score of the tournament when they were eleven. They remember the car. They remember what your face did when they opened the door. They remember whether the next fifteen minutes were the safest part of their day — or the part they learned to dread.

And here is the truth I have to put in front of you before we go one sentence further, because it's the whole chapter: your child did not get in that car asking for a coach. They got in asking for a parent. Most of us, with the best intentions in the world, hand them the wrong one.

I'm including myself. I have turned that drive into a film session more times than I want to admit. I know exactly what I'm asking you to look at, because I've had to look at it in my own mirror.

What you think you're doing, and what you're actually doing

Let's be honest about the moment, because you already know it.

The game ends. Your child climbs in, tired, emotional, the whole thing still replaying behind their eyes. And before they've even got the seatbelt on, it starts. Maybe it's the gentle version — "So what happened on that play in the third?" Maybe it's "You stopped moving your feet." Maybe you don't say a word at all, and that's worse, because the silence has a temperature, and they can feel it drop.

You tell yourself you're helping. You tell yourself a good parent doesn't just let mistakes slide, that you're teaching them to compete, that this is what investment looks like.

Here is what's actually happening. Your child is at their most raw and defenseless they will be all week, and you have chosen that exact moment to grade them. You are not correcting their footwork. You are teaching them the lesson underneath the footwork: that the warmth waiting for them depends on how they performed. That when they win, the car is a celebration, and when they lose, the car is a courtroom. You're not making them a better athlete in that moment. You're making them a more anxious one — and you're spending the one thing they needed from you that no coach, no trainer, no amount of money can ever provide.

A place to rest.

The thing they're really asking when they get quiet

Watch what your child does in that car after a hard game. They go quiet. They look out the window. And most parents read that silence as sulking, or as an opening to finally "talk about it."

It is neither. That silence is a question. They're asking — without the words, because they don't have the words yet — am I still okay? After that? Are you still glad it's me?

And whatever you do in the next sixty seconds is the answer.

If you fill it with analysis, however kind, the answer they hear is: not yet. Not until we fix this. If you fill it with disappointment, the answer is: no. And if a child gets that answer enough times, in enough cars, after enough games, they stop asking. They stop bringing you the real stuff. They learn to manage you — to give you the performance you reward and hide the parts that might cost them your warmth. You will call that "growing up" or "getting moody." It isn't. It's a child quietly deciding you are not a safe place to be human.

That is the actual price of the performance review. Not a worse athlete. A kid who stops letting you in.

The hardest version to admit

Let me name the one most of us won't say out loud.

The reason the car ride is so hard to control isn't that we don't love our kids. It's that we are still upset about the game. We watched them lose, or play scared, or get outworked, and it stirred something in us — embarrassment, frustration, our own fear about what it means. And the car becomes the place we unload that, not for their benefit, but for ours. We dress it up as coaching. It's really us, needing to feel better, using a tired twelve-year-old to do it.

I know that one from the inside. The drive home is where my own disappointment used to leak out, no matter how hard I clamped down on it, and my kid felt every degree of it before I said a word. Learning to keep my own feelings off of my child in that car was one of the hardest pieces of parenting I ever did. I'm not above this. I'm just further down the road, telling you what I wish someone had told me with the engine still running.

What to do instead — and why it costs you something

Here is the entire technique, and it's almost insultingly simple. The first words out of your mouth, win or lose, blowout or heartbreak:

"I love watching you play."

That's it. Not "great job" — that's still about performance. Not "we'll work on it" — that's still a review. Just: I love watching you play. The power is in what it refuses to do. It does not change with the scoreboard, and so it teaches your child that you do not change with the scoreboard. It cuts the wire between their performance and your love — and that wire, cut early and cut clean, is one of the greatest gifts a parent can give.

Then? Let it be quiet. Offer food. "You hungry?" Food and love is the whole menu. If they want to talk, they will, on their clock — and when they do, ask before you coach: "You want me to just listen, or do you want my take?" Then actually honor the answer, even when your take is burning a hole in your chest.

But here's the part that makes this real and not just a nice tip: doing this will cost you something. It will cost you the satisfaction of being right in the moment you most want to be right. It will mean swallowing the correction you're certain would help, watching a fixable mistake go unaddressed in the car because the relationship matters more than the footwork. It will mean letting your child be wrong, sometimes, rather than making the drive home about making them better. If you are the kind of parent who can't stand to leave a teaching moment on the table — and a lot of us are, because we care — then this will be genuinely hard. Do it anyway. The footwork can be fixed Tuesday at practice, by the coach whose job it actually is. The trust can only be built in that car, by you, and it is far easier to break than to rebuild.

If you've already gotten it wrong

Maybe you're reading this with a sinking feeling because you recognize your own car, your own face, your own ninety-second reviews. Good. That recognition is worth more than any technique, and it is not too late.

Children forgive fast when a parent goes first. You can sit your kid down and say the truest thing: "I've been treating the ride home like a coaching session, and that wasn't fair to you. That time is yours now. I'm just glad I get to watch you play." Then prove it, one quiet drive at a time. They will test it. They'll wait to see if the courtroom comes back. When it doesn't, they'll start telling you the real stuff again. That's the relationship rebuilding itself, in the front seat, where it was broken.

The rule

So here is the Coach Beede Car Ride Rule, and if you take one thing from this entire book, I'd be glad if it were this:

The car ride home belongs to your child, not to the coach in you.

Lead with "I love watching you play." Let them set the pace. Never coach uninvited from the front seat. And keep your own disappointment where it belongs — which is your problem to carry, never theirs.

Your child will remember the temperature of that drive long after they've forgotten every score. You get a few thousand of those rides, and then they're driving themselves, and the chance is gone. Don't spend them grading a kid who only ever wanted to know that you were glad it was them.

They asked for a parent. Be the parent.

Chapter 30: Advocacy or Interference?

How Parents Should Communicate With Coaches Without Hurting Their Athlete

How to Advocate Without Interfering — and Why the Athlete Should Own the Relationship Before the questions, the one rule that governs the whole chapter: as your athlete gets older, the relationship with the coach is theirs, not yours. At six, you handle everything. By high school, your athlete should be handling almost all of it, with you as the coach-of-the-advocate behind the scenes. Every answer below bends toward that handoff. A parent who's still doing all the talking to coaches when their athlete is sixteen has skipped the most valuable lesson youth sports had to teach.

And the second rule, right behind it: advocate for the experience, not the outcome. You get to care about how your athlete is treated, developed, and kept safe. You do not get to lobby for their minutes, position, or the lineup. The first is parenting. The second is interference. Almost every conversation that goes wrong crosses that line.

1. When should a parent contact a coach? Rarely, and only in the right lane. The legitimate reasons a parent contacts a coach are: safety, health, and welfare (an injury, a medical issue, a mental- health concern, a genuine wellbeing problem); logistics (schedules, conflicts, rides, a missed practice); and serious concerns about treatment (an athlete being demeaned, singled out, or unsafe). That's the lane. Stay in it.

What's not a reason to contact a coach: playing time, positions, strategy, lineup decisions, your assessment of other athletes, or your evaluation of the coach's tactics. Those belong to the coach — and increasingly to the athlete. The quick test before you hit send: Am I about to talk about my athlete's safety, health, or treatment — or about their minutes and role? The first, sometimes. The second, almost never, and never from you directly once they're old enough to do it themselves.

2. When should the athlete contact a coach? For almost everything, as soon as they're old enough — and the bar for "old enough" is lower than most parents think. By middle school an athlete can ask a coach a respectful question. By high school, the athlete should own essentially all of it: their role, their playing time, what they need to work on, a scheduling conflict, a concern about how they're being used.

This is one of the greatest gifts youth sports gives an athlete, and parents rob them of it by doing it for them. An athlete who learns to walk up to an authority figure, ask a hard question respectfully, and handle the answer like an adult has learned a skill that will pay off in every job, relationship, and hard conversation for the rest of their life. The minutes were never the point. That was the point. Let them have it.

3. What is the proper 24-hour rule? Never have a hard conversation with a coach in the heat of the moment — wait 24 hours. Right after a game,

everyone's running on adrenaline, disappointment, and raw emotion, and nothing good gets said. The 24-hour rule forces the question through a filter: do I still feel this strongly tomorrow, when I'm calm? If yes, it's probably a real concern worth raising properly. If it's evaporated by morning, it was emotion, not a concern — and you just saved a relationship.

Two refinements that make it better: praise can be immediate; concerns wait 24 hours. And the rule applies to the athlete too — teach them to cool down before they talk to a coach upset. The 24-hour rule isn't about suppressing concerns. It's about making sure the concern, not the feeling, is what gets the meeting.

4. How should a parent ask about playing time? Mostly, they shouldn't — that conversation belongs to the athlete. But if there's a version where a parent is appropriately involved (a younger athlete, or a genuine pattern worth understanding), the move is to ask about development, not minutes. Never "why isn't my athlete playing more?" Always "what does my athlete need to work on to earn more opportunity?"

That reframe changes everything. The first question is an accusation that puts a coach on defense and signals you think they're wrong. The second is a partnership that signals you trust the coach and want to help your athlete improve. One starts a fight; the other starts a plan. And the best version isn't the parent asking at all — it's the parent coaching the athlete to ask: "Coach, what do I need to do to earn more time?" That's the question that earns respect and usually earns minutes, because coaches reward athletes who ask it.

5. What should a parent never say to a coach? The relationship-killers: • "My athlete is better than [teammate]." You just made it about comparison and threw another athlete under the bus. Coaches never forget it. • "Why isn't my athlete playing?" as an accusation rather than "what can they work on?" • "You're costing my athlete a scholarship/their future." Pure pressure, usually fiction, always resented. • "I played at [level], I know better." Now you're challenging their competence. • "Other parents agree with me." Organizing a faction is the fastest way to lose a coach for good — and to mark your athlete. • Coaching the tactics — "you should run more zone." Not your lane. • Anything threatening — going to the AD, the board, social media — as a first move.

• Anything you'd be embarrassed for your athlete to hear, because they'll feel the fallout.

The filter: if it's about minutes, lineups, comparisons, or your superior knowledge, swallow it. If it's about safety, health, or genuine mistreatment, raise it calmly, privately, and 24 hours later.

6. What should a parent do if they believe the athlete is being treated unfairly? First, separate unfair treatment from a decision you don't like — they feel identical from the bleachers and they're completely different things. Not playing your athlete as much as you'd like isn't unfairness; that's a coaching decision in the coach's lane. Unfair is being demeaned, singled out, humiliated,

treated differently in a way that's about something other than the work, or anything crossing into safety or welfare. That's worth addressing.

If it's genuine: wait the 24 hours, request a private meeting (not an ambush, not a group), go in curious rather than accusatory — "Help me understand…" — and listen first; there's often context you can't see from the stands. Keep it about your athlete, never other athletes. And as they get older, bring the athlete into it or let them lead it. If after a real, calm conversation the treatment is genuinely unfair and doesn't change, that's information about whether to stay (see #19). But lead with curiosity, not the lawyer voice. Most "unfairness" dissolves with context; the real stuff reveals itself when you stay calm.

7. What should a parent do if the athlete simply needs to get better? This is the hardest and most important one, because it's the most common — and parents hate it. Often the honest answer to "why isn't my athlete playing" is just: the athlete needs to get better. Not unfairness, not politics, not a blind coach. Just not there yet.

When that's the truth, the loving move is to help them accept it and go to work — not to go hunting for a villain. Don't model "it must be someone's fault," because that teaches an athlete that setbacks are always somebody else's doing, which is a crippling life lesson. Instead: "Okay — so what do we need to get better at? Let's find out and go get it." Have the athlete ask the coach what to work on, then help them build the plan. This is where the gap is actually closed, and it's where the most valuable resilience is built.

The athlete who learns "I wasn't good enough yet, so I got better" has learned the single most useful pattern in life. Don't rob them of it by finding them an excuse.

8. How should a parent handle a coach who will not communicate? Try the proper channels first — a calm, private request for a brief conversation, in their preferred format, about something in your lane. Give it a real chance; some coaches are just bad at communication, not hostile. Coach your athlete to ask their own questions directly, which often works when parent-to-coach stalls.

But understand what chronic stonewalling tells you. A coach who won't communicate about legitimate concerns — safety, welfare, an athlete's role at an age where that's fair to ask — is showing you something about the program. Persistent, total non-communication is itself a yellow-to-red flag (it was on the fear-program list earlier in the book). You can escalate respectfully to a program director if it's a real welfare issue. But if a coach simply won't ever engage and the environment's suffering for it, that becomes part of the stay-or-go calculus — not a war to win, but data to weigh.

9. How should a parent respond if the athlete wants the parent to intervene? Resist — and coach instead. When your athlete asks you to fight their battle, the instinct is to charge in, but the more loving response is almost always: "I believe you can handle this, and I'll help you figure out how." Then actually help — role-play the conversation, work out what to say, build their courage — and send them in. You're not abandoning them; you're equipping them. The

confidence an athlete gets from handling their own hard conversation (with you in their corner) is worth ten times more than the outcome you'd have gotten by storming in.

The exceptions where a parent does step in directly: genuine safety, health, welfare, or serious mistreatment an athlete can't reasonably handle alone. Those, you handle. But "the coach isn't playing me / put me in the wrong spot / said something I didn't like" is a teach-them-to-fish moment, not a parent-charges-the-field moment. Intervene for safety. Coach for everything else.

10. What should parents avoid saying from the stands? The stands are not a coaching position, and your athlete can hear you over everyone. Avoid: • Coaching or contradicting the coach — "shoot it!" "why'd you pass?!" Now your athlete has two coaches yelling different things and can't play freely. • Yelling at officials. Teaches blame and embarrasses your athlete. • Negative reactions to your athlete's mistakes — the groan, the head-in-hands, the visible disappointment. They find that face every time. • Criticizing other athletes (or their parents are sitting right there). • Arguing calls, jawing with the other side, anything you'd be mortified to see on video.

The stands are for encouragement and presence, not instruction or judgment. The best thing your athlete should hear from the bleachers is their name and something positive — or, often, nothing at all but a calm, glad-to-be-here face. Cheer the team, stay quiet on the coaching, and save everything else for never.

11. What should parents avoid saying in group chats? The team group chat has ended more team chemistry than any losing streak. Avoid: • Playing-time and lineup complaints — it organizes discontent and always gets back to the coach. • Gossip about the coach, the program, or other athletes. • Rankings, comparisons, "what everyone else is doing" — the comparison engine again, now in text form. • Recruiting factions or parent coalitions — banding parents together against a coach marks every athlete involved. • Anything you wouldn't say to the coach's face, because functionally you just did — these things travel.

The rule: a team chat is for logistics and encouragement. The moment it becomes a venue for grievance, mute it, and never be the one who started the thread. Nothing good for your athlete has ever come out of a 10 p.m. group-chat pile-on.

12. How can parents support the coach without surrendering their responsibility as a parent? By backing the coach's authority while keeping your parental judgment. These aren't in conflict — they're a division of labor. Support looks like: not undermining the coach in front of your athlete, letting decisions you disagree with stand, reinforcing accountability ("your coach asked you to do X — let's do it"), and giving the benefit of the doubt. That's most of the time.

But supporting the coach never means surrendering your responsibility for your child's safety, health, values, and wellbeing. If a coach crosses those lines — demeaning, unsafe, pushing a hurt athlete, anything that violates your family's non-negotiables — your job as a parent overrides your support for the coach, full stop. The line is clean: back the coach on the basketball; never outsource the parenting. You can respect a coach's call on the lineup and still pull your athlete from a coach who's harming them. Authority over the sport, yes. Authority over your child's welfare, never.

13. What should an athlete say to a coach when they want more opportunity? Teach them this conversation word for word, because it's a life skill disguised as a sports skill: "Coach, I want to earn more playing time. What specifically do I need to improve to get there? I'll go to work on it."

That's it. It works because it does three things coaches love: it takes ownership (not "why aren't you playing me," but "what do I need to do"), it shows coachability, and it asks for a plan instead of a favor. Then — and this is the part — the athlete actually goes and does the work, and circles back: "Coach, I've been working on what you said. Can you tell me how I'm doing?" An athlete who runs that loop earns respect even if the minutes come slowly, and usually earns the minutes too. Almost no athletes do this. The ones who do stand out instantly.

14. What should an athlete ask if they do not understand their role? The clarity question, asked calmly and curiously:

"Coach, I want to help the team. Can you help me understand my role right now and what you need from me?"

Confusion about role breeds frustration and quiet resentment; clarity breeds buy-in. An athlete who understands exactly what's being asked — even if it's a smaller role than they want — can throw themselves into it and often grows the role by nailing it. The athlete who asks this is showing the coach maturity and team-first thinking, which is exactly the athlete coaches start trusting with more. Not knowing your role and stewing about it helps no one. Ask, understand, then own whatever it is.

15. What is the difference between advocacy and interference? Advocacy protects the experience and the person: safety, health, fair treatment, wellbeing, and — as they grow — teaching the athlete to advocate for themselves. It works with the coach and through the athlete. It asks questions and seeks understanding.

Interference tries to control the outcome: minutes, position, lineup, tactics, who plays over whom. It works against or around the coach and instead of the athlete. It makes demands and assigns blame.

The cleanest test: advocacy is about how my athlete is treated and developed; interference is about the score and the playing time. Advocacy says "is my child safe, respected, and learning?" Interference says "my child should be playing more." The first builds an athlete up and keeps the coach as an ally. The second tears the relationship down and, ironically, almost never gets the athlete more minutes — it usually gets them less.

16. What is the difference between a legitimate concern and parent frustration? Run it through three filters. Time: does it survive the 24-hour rule, or did it evaporate by morning? Frustration fades; concerns don't. Lane: is it about safety/health/treatment (legitimate) or minutes/lineup/tactics (frustration in disguise)? Pattern: is it a real, repeated pattern, or a reaction to one game, one decision, one bad day?

Legitimate concerns are durable, in-lane, and patterned. Frustration is hot, out-of-lane, and event-driven. The hard truth most parents need: the overwhelming majority of what we want to take to a coach is frustration

wearing a concern's clothes — disappointment about an outcome, dressed up as a principle. Be honest with yourself about which one you've got before you ask for the meeting. If it passes all three filters, raise it properly. If it fails any, sit with it; it's probably just the ache of watching your athlete not get what you wanted for them, which is real, but isn't the coach's problem to solve.

17. How should parents handle team politics? Mostly by refusing to play. Every team has politics — the coach's athlete, the booster's athlete, the cliques, the parent operators working angles. You will not out-politic the politics, and trying drags your athlete into a game that hurts them. The healthier path: control what you control — your athlete's work ethic, attitude, and improvement — and let that be the campaign. An athlete who's undeniably good and undeniably coachable eventually makes politics expensive to maintain.

Stay out of the parent factions. Don't be recruited into someone's coalition against a coach. Keep your athlete's head out of the adult drama. And model for them that you don't win by working the room — you win by being too good and too solid to ignore. Sometimes politics genuinely caps an athlete's opportunity in a given program, and that's real — but that's a stay-or-go question (#19), not a war to wage from the stands. You don't beat politics. You outlast it or you leave it.

18. How should parents handle favoritism? First, check whether it's favoritism or earned. Parents see the coach's athlete or the "favorite" getting more and cry favoritism, when sometimes that athlete is just better or works harder — and our love makes us bad judges of our own athlete's standing. So be honest first.

If it's real favoritism — opportunity handed out on relationships rather than merit — you still don't fix it by fighting the coach about it; that rarely changes a coach's heart and marks your athlete. You handle it the same way you handle politics: have your athlete be so good, so coachable, and so team- first that they're hard to bench, and keep their confidence intact while they outwork the favoritism. Teach them the world isn't always fair and the response to unfairness is to control your controllables and let your work argue for you. And if the favoritism is so severe that a genuinely deserving athlete is being buried and damaged by it over time — that's data for the stay-or-go decision. But the lesson you're really teaching is bigger than this team: you can't always control the favoritism, but you can make yourself undeniable.

19. When is it time to leave a team or program? Leave for the right reasons, and never teach quitting over the wrong ones.

Wrong reasons to leave: playing time you don't like, one bad season, normal adversity, a hard coach who's still fair, your athlete having to earn something. Bolting over these teaches an athlete to flee discomfort and chase the next greener field — a terrible pattern. Adversity is part of the value.

Right reasons to leave: the program is harming your athlete's safety, health, confidence, or love of the game; the coaching is genuinely abusive, demeaning, or unsafe (the fear-program red flags from earlier); the athlete is being developed poorly or not at all over a real span of time; the values clash with your family's non-negotiables; or after honest, calm attempts to address real problems, nothing changes. Those are about welfare and development, not about minutes.

The test: Are we leaving to escape adversity, or to escape harm? Escaping adversity teaches an athlete to quit. Escaping harm teaches an athlete that they matter more than a team. Know which one you're doing — and when it's genuinely harm, don't martyr your athlete to it out of loyalty or sunk cost. No banner is worth an athlete who's been damaged.

20. What should the Coach Beede Parent-Coach Communication Script say? (Full scripts in the tools below.) The heart of it: Lead with partnership, stay in your lane, wait 24 hours, ask about development not minutes, keep it private and curious, and — as they grow — put the athlete in the driver's seat. Every script in this chapter is a variation on one sentence: "How can we help my athlete grow?" — never "Why isn't my athlete getting what I want?"

Chapter Tool

The Coach Beede Parent-Coach Communication Scripts Copy-ready. Use the one that fits — and as your athlete grows, hand the script to them.

Requesting a meeting (parent): > "Coach, when you have a few minutes this week, I'd love a quick conversation about [my athlete's development / a concern]. Whatever works for you. Thanks for all you do."

The development conversation (parent, younger athlete): > "I'm not here about playing time — I trust your decisions. I just want to help. What does [athlete] need to work on to earn more opportunity, and how can we support that at home?"

Raising a genuine concern (parent, after 24 hours, private): > "Help me understand something I'm seeing — I might be missing context. [Describe the specific, in-lane concern.] I want to work with you on this. What's your read?"

The athlete asking for more opportunity (teach them this): > "Coach, I want to earn more playing time. What specifically do I need to improve? I'll go to work on it." (Then do the work, and circle back: "I've been working on what you said — how am I doing?")

The athlete asking about their role: > "Coach, I want to help the team. Can you help me understand my role right now and what you need from me?" Always: partnership over accusation · development over minutes · private over public · curious over certain · 24 hours over heat- of-the-moment · the athlete over the parent.

Advocacy vs. Interference

Advocacy
Interference
Protects the person.
Controls the outcome.
Safety, health, fair treatment, development.
Minutes, position, lineup, tactics.
Works with the coach.
Works around or against the coach.
Works through the athlete as they get older.
Works instead of the athlete.
Asks questions and seeks understanding.
Makes demands and assigns blame.
Advocacy keeps the coach an ally and builds the athlete up. Interference burns the relationship and rarely gets the minutes anyway.

Legitimate Concern vs. Frustration — 3 Filters

1. Time: Does it survive 24 hours, or did it evaporate by morning?

2. Lane: Safety / health / treatment (legit) — or minutes / lineup / tactics (frustration)?

3. Pattern: A real repeated pattern — or a reaction to one game? Concerns are durable, in-lane, and patterned. Frustration is hot, out-of-lane, and event-driven. Most of what we want to say is frustration wearing a concern's clothes.

The 24-Hour Rule Card

- Praise: immediate. Concerns: wait 24 hours.

- If you still feel it tomorrow, calmly -> it's a real concern. Raise it right.

- If it's gone by morning -> it was emotion. Let it go.

- Applies to the athlete too: cool down before talking to a coach upset.

Stay or Go — The One Question Are we leaving to escape adversity, or to escape harm? — Adversity (playing time, a hard-but-fair coach, one rough season, having to earn it) -> stay. Leaving teaches quitting. — Harm (unsafe, abusive, demeaning; joy/health/confidence being damaged; no development over real time; values violated) -> go, and don't martyr your athlete to loyalty or sunk cost.

Chapter 31: The 24-Hour Rule

How to Keep Emotion From Leading the Conversation

The 24-hour rule is the simplest tool in this entire book, and possibly the one that prevents the most damage. Here it is in two lines:

Praise can be immediate. Concerns wait 24 hours.

That's the whole rule. But the reasoning behind it, and the discipline to actually follow it, is what separates families who protect their athlete's standing from families who quietly torch it one heated conversation at a time.

Why the heat of the moment lies to you

Picture the worst possible time to make a clear-headed decision. Your athlete just got benched, or lost, or played badly, or got what felt like a raw deal from an official or a coach. Your heart is pounding. You're seeing the whole thing through disappointment, anger, fear, maybe embarrassment. The injustice feels enormous and urgent. Every cell in your body wants to do something right now — fire off the text, corner the coach in the parking lot, demand an explanation.

That moment, right there, is when more parent-coach relationships get destroyed than at any other time. Because the version of you that exists ninety seconds after a tough game is not the version that should be representing your family. You're not thinking; you're reacting. And reactions sent in the heat of the moment can't be unsent.

The same is true for everyone else in that parking lot. The coach is emotional. The other parents are emotional. Your athlete is emotional. Putting a hard conversation into that environment is like trying to defuse something delicate while everyone's hands are shaking.

What the rule actually does

The 24-hour rule isn't about silencing your concerns or pretending you don't have them. It's a filter. It forces every concern to answer one question before it gets a meeting: do I still feel this strongly tomorrow, when I'm calm?

If you do — if you wake up the next morning and the concern is still there, clear-eyed and steady — then it's probably a real concern, and you should raise it properly: calmly, privately, in the right lane. The rule didn't stop you.

It just made sure the concern, not the emotion, is what shows up to the conversation.

But here's what happens most of the time: by morning, it's gone. The fury that felt like a principle the night before turns out to have been frustration — the ache of watching your athlete not get what you wanted for them. And you just saved a relationship you'd have damaged over a feeling that evaporated overnight. That's the rule doing its quietest, most important work.

It belongs to the athlete too

This rule isn't just for parents. Teach it to your athlete, because they need it just as much. A high school athlete who's upset after a game should never confront a coach in the heat of it — that's how an athlete burns a bridge with the person who controls their playing time. Teach them to cool down, think, prepare, and then speak with maturity if it still matters tomorrow.

This is one of those places where a sports lesson is secretly a life lesson. The adult who can sit with a strong feeling for a day before responding — instead of firing off the angry email, the heated text, the words they can't take back — has a superpower in work, in marriage, in every hard conversation life will hand them. You're not just protecting their standing on the team. You're teaching them how to be a person who responds instead of reacts.

The goal is wisdom, not silence

Let me be clear about what this rule is not. It is not a gag order. It does not mean parents and athletes should swallow real concerns and never speak up. Safety, health, genuine mistreatment — some things deserve a calm, prompt conversation, and the rule never asks you to bury those.

The goal of the 24-hour rule is not silence. The goal is wisdom. It's making sure that when you do speak, it's your wisest self talking and not your most wounded self. It's the difference between a concern that improves a situation and a reaction that blows one up.

So before you send the text, before you find the coach, before you let a raw moment write a message you'll regret — wait a day. Praise can't wait; tell your athlete you loved watching them play right now. But concerns can wait, and they should. If it still matters tomorrow, raise it well. If it's gone by morning, let it go, and be grateful you didn't send it.

The 24-hour rule makes sure the concern, not the emotion, gets the meeting.

Chapter Tool

(See full tool in the Parent Toolkit Appendix.)

Chapter 32: What to Say to a Coach

Scripts for Playing Time, Role, Development, and Genuine
Concerns Most parents don't damage their athlete's standing with a coach
on purpose. They do it with the wrong sentence, said with the best intentions, in
the wrong lane. So this chapter is practical: the actual words to use, and the ones
to bury, when you communicate with a coach.

But before the scripts, the two rules that govern all of them — because a
script in the wrong spirit still backfires.

Rule one: stay in your lane. You get to care about how your athlete is treated,
developed, and kept safe. You do not get to lobby for their minutes, position, or
the lineup. The first is parenting; the second is interference, and coaches can
smell the difference instantly. Almost every conversation that goes wrong
crosses that line.

Rule two: as they grow, hand the conversation to the athlete. The single
most powerful version of nearly every script below isn't you saying it — it's you
coaching your athlete to say it. By high school, the athlete should own almost
all of this. A college coach told me once what he looks for on a visit, and it
stuck with me: he watches whether the recruit or the parent answers his
questions. One of those athletes helps his own recruitment. The other quietly
ends it. Coaches notice who drives the conversation. Make sure, more and more,
it's your athlete.

Requesting a conversation

Open with partnership, never ambush: "Coach, when you have a few minutes
this week, I'd appreciate a quick conversation about my athlete's development.
Whatever works for you. Thank you for everything you do."

Notice what that does: it's low-pressure, it names a lane (development), it
respects their time, and it opens with gratitude. A coach who gets that message
isn't on the defensive before you've even sat down.

The development conversation (the playing-time question, done right)

This is the big one, because playing time is what parents most want to raise
and most often raise badly. The wrong version — "Why isn't my athlete playing
more?" — is an accusation. It tells the coach you think they're wrong and puts
them on defense. The right version reframes it entirely: "I'm not here about
playing time — I trust your decisions. I just want to help. What does my athlete
need to work on to earn more opportunity, and how can we support that at
home?"

Same underlying concern, opposite reception. One starts a fight; the other
starts a plan. And the best version is the one your athlete delivers: (Athlete)
"Coach, I want to earn more playing time. What specifically do I need to
improve? I'll go to work on it."

Then — this is the part that matters — the athlete actually does the work and circles back: "Coach, I've been working on what you said. How am I doing?" An athlete who runs that loop earns respect even when the minutes come slowly, and usually earns the minutes too. Almost no athletes do this. The ones who do stand out immediately.

The role conversation

When an athlete is confused or frustrated about their role, confusion curdles into resentment unless it's replaced with clarity. Teach them to ask: (Athlete) "Coach, I want to help the team. Can you help me understand my role right now and what you need from me?"

An athlete who understands their role — even a smaller one than they want — can throw themselves into it and often grows it by nailing it. Asking this question signals maturity and team-first thinking, which is exactly the athlete coaches start trusting with more.

The genuine concern (after 24 hours, private, curious)

When there's a real, in-lane concern — treatment, safety, welfare — raise it the right way: cooled down, in private, with curiosity instead of accusation:

"Help me understand something I'm seeing — I might be missing context. [Describe the specific concern.] I want to work with you on this. What's your read?"

"Help me understand" is the most disarming opening in the language. It assumes you might not have the full picture (you usually don't, from the stands), and it invites the coach to be a partner rather than a defendant.

What to bury

Never say: "My athlete is better than [teammate]." "Why isn't my athlete playing?" as an accusation. "You're costing my athlete a scholarship." "I played at [level], I know better." "Other parents agree with me." Anything coaching the tactics. Anything threatening the AD, the board, or social media as a first move. And nothing you'd be embarrassed for your athlete to overhear — because they'll feel the fallout of every one of those sentences.

The filter is simple: if it's about minutes, lineups, comparisons, or your superior knowledge, swallow it. If it's about safety, health, or genuine mistreatment, raise it — calmly, privately, and a day later. Get the lane right and the words right, and you'll keep the coach an ally instead of making them an obstacle.

Chapter Tool

(See full tool in the Parent Toolkit Appendix.)

Chapter 33: Legitimate Concern or Parent Frustration?

Frustration?
The Difference Matters Not every strong feeling is a legitimate concern. That sentence might be the most useful thing in this entire part of the book, because the single most common mistake parents make with coaches is taking frustration into a meeting dressed up as a concern — and not even knowing they've done it.

The two feel identical from the bleachers. Both are intense. Both come from love. Both make you want to do something. But they're completely different things, and treating one like the other is how good parents damage their

athlete's standing while believing they're advocating for them. So you need a way to tell them apart before you act.

What each one actually is

A legitimate concern is durable, in-lane, and patterned. It survives 24 hours. It involves safety, health, treatment, development, or genuine wellbeing. And it shows up more than once — it's a real pattern, not a single bad moment. A coach who's consistently demeaning an athlete, a safety issue that keeps recurring, a welfare problem that doesn't resolve: those are concerns. They're worth a calm, private conversation.

Parent frustration is hot, out-of-lane, and event-driven. It flares up after a specific game, a specific benching, a specific decision you didn't like. It's almost always about playing time, lineup, tactics, role, comparison — or, underneath all of those, the simple pain of watching your athlete not get what you hoped they'd get.

And here's the part I need you to hear clearly: that pain is real. I'm not dismissing it. Watching your child sit when you know how hard they worked, or lose a spot, or not get the role you believe they deserve — that aches, and the ache is legitimate as a feeling. But a real feeling is not the same as a real concern, and it is not always the coach's problem to solve. Most of the disappointment of youth sports isn't a problem to be fixed. It's a hard thing to be felt, and moved through.

The three filters

Before you contact a coach about anything, run the feeling through three questions. Be honest, because the whole value is in the honesty.
Time: Does this still matter 24 hours from now, when I'm calm? Frustration fades by morning. Concerns don't.

Lane: Is this about safety, health, treatment, or development — or is it about minutes, lineup, tactics, and role? The first lane is yours to raise. The second isn't, and it belongs increasingly to the athlete anyway.

Pattern: Is this a real, repeated pattern — or am I reacting to one game, one decision, one bad day? One data point is rarely a concern. A pattern is.

If the answer is yes to all three — durable, in-lane, patterned — raise it, calmly and privately, using the scripts from the last chapter. If it fails any of

the three, pause. It's almost certainly frustration, and frustration taken to a coach doesn't help your athlete. It marks them.

The honest mirror

Here's the uncomfortable truth that makes this chapter matter: most of what parents want to say to a coach is frustration wearing a concern's clothes. We feel the sting of our athlete's disappointment, and our mind immediately dresses it up as a principle — "this isn't fair," "the coach doesn't see him," "this is hurting her development" — because "I'm upset my athlete isn't playing" feels too small to act on, while "this is a legitimate concern" feels worthy of a meeting.

The three filters

are a mirror. They force you to look honestly at which one you've actually got before you act on it. And learning to sit with frustration without converting it into a coach confrontation is one of the most protective things you can do for your athlete — because every time you take frustration to a coach as if it were a concern, you spend a little of your athlete's standing, and you teach your athlete that disappointment is something someone else has to fix.

So before you act: is this durable, in-lane, and patterned? If yes, you have a concern — handle it well. If no, you have frustration — feel it, let it settle, and let it go. The difference matters more than almost anything else in how you'll be received, and in what you're teaching your athlete about handling the hard parts.

Chapter Tool

(See full tool in the Parent Toolkit Appendix.)

Chapter 34: Stay or Go?

Escaping Harm Without Teaching Athletes to Run From Adversity

Every family eventually faces the hardest question in youth sports: should we stay, or should we go?

It comes in many forms. A coach you've lost faith in. A program that isn't what it promised. A role your athlete can't seem to climb out of. A culture that feels off. A better-looking opportunity across town waving at you. And

the decision feels impossibly tangled — until you realize it all comes down to a single distinction that cuts cleanly through every version of it:

Are we leaving to escape adversity, or to escape harm?

Get that distinction right, and the answer usually reveals itself. Get it wrong, and you either teach your athlete to quit every time things get hard, or you martyr them to a situation that's genuinely damaging them. Both are serious mistakes, in opposite directions.

Adversity is supposed to be there

Adversity is a normal, valuable, non-negotiable part of sports. A hard coach who's demanding but fair. A role that has to be earned and hasn't been yet. A rough season. A difficult teammate. A competitive environment where your athlete isn't the star. A stretch where the honest truth is that they simply need to get better.

None of that is a reason to leave. In fact, that's the value. The athlete who learns to handle a tough-but-fair coach, to earn a role instead of being handed it, to push through a rough season without bailing — that athlete is building the exact resilience the sport exists to build. Leaving every time it gets hard teaches the single most dangerous lesson youth sports can teach: that the response to difficulty is to flee to an easier situation.

I've watched families program-hop chasing comfort, switching teams every time their athlete hit friction, and the pattern they built into their child was unmistakable by high school — at the first sign of adversity, look for the exit. That's not a sports problem. That's a life problem you've rehearsed into them. Healthy adversity asks the athlete to grow. It should not train the family to bolt the moment a season gets hard.

Harm is different — and you don't wait it out

Harm is a different category entirely, and the same toughness that says "don't quit over adversity" must not be twisted into "endure harm out of loyalty."

Harm is an unsafe environment. Abusive or genuinely demeaning coaching — shame and humiliation dressed up as toughness. An athlete's joy, confidence, or health being actively damaged over time. A program that ignores injuries or pushes a hurt athlete to play. A culture that violates your family's core values. A fear-based environment that's making your athlete smaller, quieter, and more afraid month over month.

When it's genuinely harm, you go. And you don't martyr your athlete to loyalty, to sunk cost, to the money you've already spent, or to a logo. No banner, no team, no relationship with a coach is worth a child who's being damaged. The sunk cost is the trap here — "we've put so much into this program" is the exact reasoning that keeps families in harmful situations long past when they should have walked. What you've already spent is gone either way. The only question is what's best for the athlete now.

The test, and the courage to use it

So when you're agonizing over whether to stay or go, strip away the noise and ask the one question: Is this adversity, or is this harm?

Adversity builds. Harm damages. Escaping adversity teaches your athlete to quit; escaping harm teaches your athlete that they matter more than a team. Know which one you're actually dealing with — and be honest, because frustration (the last chapter) loves to disguise itself as harm to justify a move you wanted to make anyway.

If it's adversity, stay, and help your athlete grow through it. That's where the gold is. If it's genuinely harm, go, and don't let loyalty or sunk cost keep your child in a place that's hurting them. The courage to tell the difference — and to act on it cleanly — is one of the most important things a sports parent ever has to do.

Chapter Tool

(See full tool in the Parent Toolkit Appendix.)

Chapter 35: The Courage to Say No

When the Best Decision Is to Step Back

Everything in youth sports is engineered to get you to say yes. The whole machine is a chorus of yes — yes to the extra team, yes to the showcase, yes to the trainer, yes to the year-round commitment, yes to the can't-miss opportunity. And the hardest, rarest, most protective word a sports parent owns is the one nobody's selling:

No.

Not yet. Not this one. Not at this price. Not at this age. Not while we're already exhausted. No. And I want to make the case that saying it — at the right moments, for the right reasons — takes more courage and does more good than almost any yes you'll ever say.

Why no is so hard

No is hard because the entire environment punishes it. Say no to the extra team and you watch another family say yes and feel the fear tighten. Say no to the showcase and the voice in your head whispers that this was the one. Say no and you risk being the parent who "didn't do everything," who "held their athlete back," who wasn't "committed." Every yes feels like love and proof of commitment. Every no feels like neglect and risk.

But that's exactly backwards, and recognizing it is the heart of this chapter. In an environment built to extract endless yeses, no is often the more loving and more committed choice. The parent who can say no is the parent protecting the athlete's rest, the family's rhythm, the bank account, the joy, and the long game — against a machine that would happily consume all of them one reasonable yes at a time.

What I tell families who've already spent thirty thousand dollars

I've sat with a lot of families who are deep in — who've spent enormous money, given up years of weekends, said yes to everything, and find themselves with a tired athlete, a drained account, and a creeping sense that something went wrong. And the hardest thing I have to tell them is that the next right move is almost never another yes. It's a no. The biggest mistake families make isn't doing too little. It's doing too much — every showcase, every camp, every team — until they've produced an exhausted athlete and an empty bank account.

The courage to say no is the courage to stop the bleed. To look at a packed calendar and remove something. To skip the event everyone's going to. To take the off-season the culture says you can't afford. To let your athlete be bored on a Saturday. None of that feels like progress in a world that measures love in activity. All of it is, because less, chosen on purpose, is how you protect the things that actually make an athlete: rest, joy, health, and a family that still likes each other.

No is a complete sentence

Parents tie themselves in knots trying to justify every no — explaining, apologizing, softening, as if declining an opportunity requires a doctor's note. It doesn't. "Not yet" is a complete sentence. "That doesn't work for our family this season" is a complete sentence. You don't owe the showcase organizer, the club director, or the loudest parent in the group chat a defense of your family's choices.

And the no doesn't have to be forever. Most of the time it's simply not now — not at this age, not this season, not while the family's running on fumes, not until the athlete actually asks for it. A no today preserves the option of a yes later, when it might actually fit. That's not closing a door. That's refusing to walk through every door someone else opens just because it's open.

Stepping back as strength

Sometimes the bravest thing a parent does is step back entirely — pull back from the chase, lower the temperature, let the athlete breathe, let the family reset. The culture will read that as falling behind. It isn't. It's the family whose athlete still has fresh legs and a full heart when the "more" families have burned out and quit.

Saying no, stepping back, choosing less — these aren't signs that you care less. They're signs you've decided to care about the right things, and to defend them against a machine that profits from your yes. As the spine of this whole book puts it: you will not let fear make the plan. And fear's favorite word is yes. Reclaim the no, use it with courage, and you protect everything that matters most.

Chapter Tool

(See full tool in the Parent Toolkit Appendix.)

Part VII — The Long Game

Chapter 36: The 40-Year Plan

We Are Raising Adults Who Happened to Be Athletes

Almost everyone in youth sports is running a four-year plan. Get to varsity. Get recruited. Get the offer. Get to college. Four years of vision, and the whole family quietly bends itself around it — the calendar, the budget, the dinner conversations, the mood in the house on a Sunday night.

I've come to coach by a different number. Forty years.

The forty-year plan asks one question of every decision: where is this child at forty? Not at eighteen — at forty. Because here is the arithmetic almost no one in this industry will do with you. Even the rare child who makes it all the way to college sports is finished competing by their early twenties. A handful of years. And then they have another sixty to be a person — a husband, a wife, a parent, an employee, a boss, a neighbor, a friend, someone who has to get up on an ordinary Monday and carry an ordinary life with some measure of grace.

So the forty-year plan says the thing that should reorganize how you make every single decision in this whole endeavor: you are not raising a college athlete. You are raising a forty-year-old. The sport is one of the finest tools you will ever be handed for that work — but it was always the tool, and never the thing itself.

What's actually in the box at forty

Be honest with yourself about what survives.

The trophies are in a box in the basement, and your child will not open it. The rankings stopped mattering the week after they were posted. The highlight clips are buried somewhere on an old phone. And the athletic career — for all but a vanishing few, and even for them, only briefly — is over by an age when most people are just getting started at life.

So what's left? What did all of it actually build?

The discipline. The resilience. The particular strength of a person who has lost in front of everyone and gotten back up anyway. The ease in their own body. The knowledge, carried in the bones, that hard things can be survived and that effort in the dark eventually shows up in the light. My own father gave me those things without ever making a speech about them — he taught with his hands and his example: work, responsibility, showing up when you don't feel like it. Work in silence. Stack days. Let the work show up when it is ready.

That is what's in the box at forty. Not the medals. The person the medals were quietly forging the whole time. The four-year plan optimizes for the offer. The forty-year plan optimizes for the human being who has to live the next sixty years — and the staggering thing, the thing I have watched break a thousand families' hearts, is that you do not have to choose between them. The forty-year human and the eighteen-year-old athlete are built by the same things. Joy. Health. A relationship that survives the hard seasons. A childhood that wasn't spent entirely in a uniform. Pursue those, and you very often get the athlete and the adult. Sacrifice them chasing the offer, and you frequently lose both.

The turn

Now I want to turn this around, because the whole book until now has shown you what your fear can cost your child — the joy it dims, the trust it spends, the body it wears down, the childhood it quietly consumes. That was the hard half. Here is the half I most wanted you to reach.

When you put the fear down — when you stop coaching the outcome and start raising the human — something comes back to you.

Look at who your child gets to become when you get this right. Not an anxious performer scanning the stands for your approval, but a young person who competes because they love it, fails without shattering, owns their own dream, and walks toward their future under their own power. A kid who calls home from college not because they have to report a result, but because they actually want to talk to you. An adult, someday, who brings their own children to you and says: my mom, my dad — they made it fun. They made me feel like more than a scoreboard. They're the reason I still love this. That is the child waiting on the other side of your fear. Not a lesser athlete. A whole one.

But here is the part nobody tells the parent, the warmest thing I know in all of this: you get someone back too.

You get to stop being the manager, the critic, the anxious investor doing math at midnight, and go back to being something far better and far rarer — a fan. A parent in the stands who is simply, uncomplicatedly delighted that this person exists and that you get to watch them play. The relief of it is almost physical. When you stop carrying the outcome — an outcome you could never actually control anyway, no matter how much you spent or how hard you pushed — you can finally feel the weight of what you've been holding, because it's gone. You get to enjoy your child again. You get the Saturdays back. You get the dinners back. You get the relationship back. You get to be the parent you actually wanted to be before the fear talked you into someone harder and smaller.

That is the redemption hiding inside the forty-year plan. It was never only about protecting your child from your fear. It was about freeing you from it.

The seats I've sat in

I have watched this game from every chair there is — as the athlete, as the college coach reading recruits across a desk, as the advisor at a thousand kitchen tables, and as a father in the very seat you're sitting in now, with all the fear that comes with it. I'm not writing to you from above any of this. I have wanted the outcome too badly. I have done the midnight math. I have had to learn, the slow way, the difference between loving a child and managing one.

And the one thing all those chairs taught me, the thing I would carry back and tell my younger self with the gear bag by the door, is this: the sport was never the point. It was the vehicle. The point was always the person riding in it

— the human being your child is becoming, and the parent you get to be alongside them.

So build your whole philosophy on this one line: we are not in the business of building athletes. We are in the business of raising adults who happened to be athletes. The sport is a magnificent door. But a door is for walking through, into a life on the other side that is so much larger than any game. The day the sport stops being a door into that larger life and becomes the entire house your child is trapped inside, you've traded sixty years for four — and you've traded the parent you could have been for one the fear invented.

Play the long game. Raise the forty-year-old. The athlete is the shape your child takes for a while on the way to becoming themselves — and you get the gift of a lifetime, which is the chance to watch it happen, and to be loved by who they become.

I learned that lesson as a father in a way no theory could have taught me. In August of 2011, Tyler faced the kind of decision every baseball family thinks it wants until it is actually sitting in the room with you: sign professionally or go to Vanderbilt. The clock was real. The money was real. The pressure was real. Every practical voice in the world had an argument to make, and none of them were small.

But underneath all of it was the bigger question. Not just where would he pitch next, but who would this decision help him become? Vanderbilt was not only a uniform. It was a campus, a coach, a classroom, teammates, standards, pressure, independence, and a life he could not fully see yet. He chose the life. Three years later, when he was drafted in the first round again after winning a national championship and growing inside that environment, it would have been easy to make the story about baseball. It was bigger than that. The college decision had given him years no signing bonus could have recreated: relationships, maturity, ownership, and a chapter of life that shaped the man as much as the pitcher.

That is the 40-year plan in a real room, with real pressure on it. The right choice is not always the loudest one or the richest one or the one the outside world understands fastest. Sometimes the right choice is the one that gives the young person more room to become.

And because life is never done testing what it built, the years keep moving. Uniforms change. Roles change. Cities change. Bodies age. Children grow up, leave home, build families of their own, and one day grandchildren run through rooms and across ballfields with no idea what was protected, sacrificed, or survived so that ordinary could feel ordinary to them.

Maybe that is the truest measure of grace: what one generation carries with effort can become, for the next, simply the floor beneath their feet.

Eligibility Strategy Is Not Life Strategy

A practical warning lives inside this, because the forty-year plan has a counterfeit, and families fall for it constantly.

Eligibility matters. Rules matter. Timelines matter. Understand them. But do not let eligibility strategy quietly take over your life strategy. The real question was never only how many years of eligibility a child can preserve, gain, time, or delay. The real question is what path gives this young person the best chance to succeed as a student, as a human being, and as an athlete — in that order.

A family can get so consumed with banking a year, gaining a year, timing a year, that they forget to ask what the years are actually for. College is not an athletic holding room. It is the doorway into adulthood — where a young person learns to live away from home, manage their time, sit in hard classes, recover from disappointment, advocate for themselves, and start building the life they'll live long after the sport stops paying attention. For nearly every athlete, the sport will not pay the bills past their early twenties. That isn't pessimism. It's arithmetic, and it's the same arithmetic the whole chapter rests on. So the path has to serve the life, not just the eligibility clock.

Eligibility is a rule. Life is the plan. Never confuse the two.

Chapter Tool

(See full tool in the Parent Toolkit Appendix — the 40-Year Plan Gut Check.)

Chapter 37: Academics Are Development

What Grades Reveal About Habits, Maturity, and Time

Here's a sentence that should reorganize how your family treats school: the classroom is the one arena where almost every athlete will still be competing at forty. The field has an expiration date. The mind does not. But "education matters" is a bumper sticker, and kids tune it out — so let me make the case in a way that actually connects to everything else in this book.

Academics are not separate from athletic development. They are athletic development. The same engine that builds a great athlete builds a strong student, and treating the two as enemies — treating school as the boring thing competing with the sport — is one of the most expensive mistakes a sports family makes. And I want to name who usually makes it: it's the parent who says "school comes first" and then organizes the entire calendar, budget, and dinner conversation around the sport, and wonders why the kid got the message that school was the thing you do after the thing that matters. Children believe what we prioritize, not what we announce.

Grades aren't about intelligence

The first thing to understand is that grades are rarely a measure of how smart a kid is. They're a report card on habits. A transcript tells a coach — and tells you — whether this athlete can manage time, meet a deadline, deal with an authority figure they don't love, do work they don't feel like doing, and own it when they fall short. Read that list again: time management, discipline, dealing with authority, doing the unglamorous work nobody's clapping for, accountability. Those are the exact traits that make a great athlete. The kid who can grind through a brutal conditioning block can grind through a chemistry unit — it's the same muscle, pointed at a different target.

So when grades slip on a talented athlete, it's almost never an intelligence problem. It's a priorities problem or a support problem — and both are fixable, and both are the parent's department, not the coach's. This is exactly why college coaches care about grades far past the eligibility math. An athlete who handles the classroom is an athlete who'll handle the playbook, the curfew, and the 6 a.m. lift. The transcript is a preview of how a kid will handle the whole of the next level.

Grades expand the path — they don't compete with it

I've watched a transcript open a door an athlete's ability alone couldn't — and I've watched one quietly close a door that should have stayed open.

I think of a softball player named Erin Scanlan. Erin was a good high school athlete — genuinely good, but not the kind of dominant, can't-miss recruit that programs build a class around. On the field alone, the most competitive academic schools might have been just out of reach. What set Erin apart wasn't

154

her ceiling as a player. It was her discipline in the classroom, and it was relentless.

That discipline showed up on a transcript that did exactly what this chapter has been describing: it told every coach and every admissions office that here was a young woman who managed her time, met her deadlines, did the hard work whether she felt like it or not, and held herself accountable. And that transcript opened a door her athletic résumé alone might not have. She got into Holy Cross — a serious academic school in a serious conference — and in a real sense she traded up. She used her grades to turn good-not-dominant softball into an opportunity at a school that mattered for the next forty years, not just the next four.

Here's the part I want every parent to sit with. Erin went on to become a doctor at Children's Hospital in Boston. Softball was the platform — it got her onto a campus and into a life — but it was her habits, the ones her transcript had been quietly advertising the whole time, that carried her into a career that will outlast any season she ever played. The grades were never separate from the athlete. They were the truest preview of the adult.

Coaches read a transcript as a forecast, not a formality. The grades were never just about school.

Here's the reframe that takes the punishment out of the whole school conversation. Most families frame academics as the thing that takes away the sport: drop the grades, lose eligibility, off the team. That makes school the enemy of the thing the kid loves — and kids fight enemies. Flip it. Grades don't limit the sports path. They widen it. A strong athlete with weak grades has a narrow funnel — only the programs that can carry the academic risk, only as long as the body holds. A good athlete with strong grades can walk through almost any door: the academic-minded program, the school where merit aid makes the money work, the place that turns them down athletically but wants the whole package. Good grades make an athlete easier to recruit, not harder, because they signal lower risk and can free up a coach's athletic budget with academic money.

So school isn't standing between your athlete and the dream. It's what gives the dream more doors. Same energy you'd bring to the weight room — you don't call that punishment, you call it the thing that makes you better. School is reps for the brain, and it widens the future.

The insurance that never lapses

And here is the deepest reason academics are development: they're the one part of the plan no injury can take away. One torn knee, one growth plate that won't cooperate, one coaching change, one of the thousands of roster spots that simply vanish — the athletic plan can end in a single afternoon, with no warning and no appeal. The academic plan can't be taken by a hit or a cut. When you make grades matter as much as the game, you are buying the only insurance policy in youth sports that never lapses.

So stop using school and sport as punishments for each other — no benching for a bad grade, no extra studying as penance for a bad game. That teaches a child the two are at war, when your whole job is to show them they're teammates. The work ethic to do this already lives in your athlete; they prove it every time they train. The job is simply to point that same discipline at the classroom and to stop treating school like the consolation prize. It isn't the consolation prize. It's the main prize, wearing a disguise — and the parent who can't see that is mortgaging a forty-year mind to protect a four-year game.

Chapter Tool

The Transcript-as-Forecast Check

Look at your athlete's transcript the way a college coach will — not for the grade, but for what it forecasts. Does it show they can manage their time? Meet deadlines? Take instruction from someone they don't love? Recover from a bad mark? Do the unglamorous work? Then ask the parent questions: Am I treating school as opportunity or as punishment? Does my family's calendar say school matters, or just my speeches? If the sport ended tomorrow, would my child's transcript open doors or close them?

The grades were never about being smart. They're a forecast of the adult — and everyone recruiting your child is reading the forecast, whether you are or not.

Chapter 38: Fit Before Level

Why the Right School Beats the Biggest Logo

When it finally comes time to choose where an athlete plays at the next level, families make one mistake more than any other, and it's expensive in every way that matters: they shop for level when they should be shopping for fit.

Level is the label — the division, the highest tier that'll take your athlete, the most impressive logo on the hat. Fit is whether your athlete will actually thrive there, play, develop, graduate, and walk out a better human after four years. Level flatters the parent. Fit serves the athlete. And the gap between those two things is where a lot of young athletes end up miserable, transferring, or quietly walking away from a sport they used to love.

What "fit" actually means

Let me give you the definition I've given recruiting families for years, because it cuts through all the logo-worship: fit isn't the school's name. Fit is whether your athlete can succeed academically, contribute athletically, and grow personally for four years. If two of those three aren't true, it's not a fit — no matter what hat is on the table.

Sit with that, because it reorders everything. The famous program where your athlete won't see the field, can't keep up in the classroom, and is miserable in the culture is a worse choice than the lesser-known school where they play, thrive academically, and are happy — even though the hat is less impressive. The logo plays four games a year on television. The fit lives with your athlete every single day for four years.

The layers of fit, in order

Fit has layers, and you weigh them roughly in this order — with level coming last, not first:

Academic fit. Does this school have the major and the academic support the athlete actually needs? Could they succeed here if they never played a down? If not, the level is irrelevant — you're building on sand.

Financial fit. What's the real net cost after all aid — athletic, academic, need-based? The "lower" school that costs the family almost nothing can be the best decision you ever make. (More on this in the next chapter — the math surprises people.)

Culture fit. Will this athlete be happy in this locker room, with this coach, in this town, for four years? Culture determines whether they last, and almost nobody evaluates it because they're dazzled by the brand. Here's the test I give families: watch how the coach treats his current players when nobody's recruiting, watch how he talks about the players who left, watch how his current parents describe him. The culture is already on display. Look at it honestly.

Environment fit. Campus size and geography, matched to this specific athlete. A homebody at a giant school eight hours from home can drown. An athlete who needs energy and anonymity can wither at a tiny school twenty minutes away. Match the environment to the actual human, not the brochure.

Playing fit. Will they actually play, develop, and matter to this team — or be roster insurance? An athlete who plays and grows at a "lower" level develops more than an athlete who rots on the bench at a "higher" one. Reps build athletes. Benches build resentment.

Level. Only now, last, after all of that: which division do the surviving options happen to be? Nine times out of ten, the right fit is a "lower" level than the parent's ego wanted — and a far better four years than the ego would have gotten.

The illusion the level chase sells

The reason families chase level over fit is that level is visible and fit is felt. You can post the logo. You can tell the relatives the division. You can win the conversation at the holiday table. Fit doesn't photograph well — but it's the thing that determines whether your athlete is happy, playing, graduating, and grateful, or transferring twice and leaving without a degree.

I've watched the level chase wreck good outcomes too many times: the athlete who took the bigger offer over the better fit and spent two miserable years on a bench before transferring down to exactly the kind of school they

could have started at as a freshman. The level flattered everyone for one signing-day photo. The fit would have given them four good years.

So run the fit filters first — academics, money, culture, environment, playing time — and let level be the last thing you check, not the first. Recruit the fit, not the logo. The logo fades by sophomore year. The fit is the four years your athlete actually lives.

Recruitability Is Level-Specific Recruitability is not universal.

An athlete may not be recruitable at one level and may be an excellent fit at another. That is not failure. That is information.

The question is not, "Is my athlete recruitable?"

The better question

is, "At what level, in what environment, and for what kind of program is my athlete truly a fit?"

A coach at one level may see a limitation. A coach at another may see a cornerstone. A school with one academic profile may be wrong. Another may be a perfect match. A program with one roster need may pass. Another may value exactly what the athlete brings.

This is why fit comes before level.

A realistic fit gives the athlete a chance to play, grow, graduate, and become. The wrong level can flatter the parent while quietly burying the athlete.

Start With the Schools That Are Actually Interested Parents often begin with the schools they want.

A more useful starting point is the schools that are interested.

Every college coach who takes the time to call, email, text, visit, evaluate, or express genuine interest is giving your athlete something valuable: a possible doorway. It may not be the logo your family imagined. It may not be the level that flatters the parent. It may not be the school that looks best in a social media post.

But interest matters.

A real coach at a real school who sees value in your athlete is not something to dismiss because the label is not exciting enough. That coach may understand the fit better than the family does. That school may offer the right academic path, the right social environment, the right playing opportunity, the right financial package, and the right transition into adulthood.

Every level of college athletics can be a win if it is the right fit.

Listen early to the schools that show sincere interest. Ask better questions. Compare the full experience. Look at academics, geography, culture, roster opportunity, cost, support, and the athlete's own excitement.

The goal is not to win the announcement.

The goal is to build the right four-year life.

Chapter Tool

(See full tool in the Parent Toolkit Appendix.)

Chapter 39: Scholarships, Reality, and the Net Cost

Why Athletic Money Should Be a Bonus, Not the Plan

Let me say the thing the youth sports industry will never put on a flyer, because it's the most important financial truth a sports family will ever hear: for the overwhelming majority of families, the athletic scholarship is not a plan. It's a long shot you should never be funding your child's college on.

I don't say that to crush a dream. I say it because I've watched too many families pour money, weekends, and years into chasing athletic money that, by the numbers, was never likely to come — while ignoring the surer, larger, more reliable money sitting right next to it. The whole calculation is usually backwards, and getting it right can save a family tens of thousands of dollars and a lot of heartache.

The numbers nobody wants to hear

Here's the reality. Athletic scholarships go to a tiny fraction of high school athletes — well under two in a hundred get any athletic money at all. Full rides are rarer still, around one percent, and they cluster in a short list of sports. The "athletic ability will pay for college" plan simply does not happen for the vast majority of families who bank on it.

And even when athletic money comes, it's widely misunderstood. Most athletic scholarships are partial — a slice of one sport's limited pot, divided across a roster. An athlete might get a quarter of the cost covered and the family writes a check for the rest. The average award is often modest, sometimes less than the academic or need-based aid a strong student could have gotten with no sport at all. And it's typically year-to-year — it has to be re-earned, and a new coach owes the old coach's promises nothing.

The recruiting landscape recently got harder for the average recruit, not easier. The rules changed in a way that compressed rosters and squeezed exactly the developmental and walk-on spots that the "raw potential" athlete used to grow into. So there's more money concentrated at the very top, and fewer doors in the middle — the opposite of what most families assume when they hear that athletes can get paid now.

The math that flips it

Here's where it gets practical and a little surprising. Families write off the "no athletic scholarship" schools — Division III, the academically elite programs — as not worth it. That's exactly backwards.

A Division III school with strong merit aid can cost a family less than a Division I school offering a small partial athletic scholarship. I've run this math with families more times than I can count, and the ranking nobody sees is on the cost-of-attendance line. The school that gives zero athletic money but generous academic aid often comes out cheaper and offers better playing time, better development, and a better academic experience. The "non- scholarship" school is frequently the cheaper school. You just have to do the math on the net cost — what you actually pay after all aid — instead of getting hypnotized by the word "scholarship."

This is why the previous two chapters matter so much here. A strong transcript is a more reliable scholarship than a strong jump shot, because academic and need-based aid is available to far more athletes, at far more schools, and often in larger amounts than the athletic money would have been.

How to actually fund it

So here's the honest guidance I give every family: don't fund your athlete's college on their athletic ability. Fund it on their transcript, their financial-aid forms, and a clear-eyed look at the real net price of each school. Treat any athletic money that comes as a bonus — a nice addition to a plan that was already sound — never as the plan itself.

Chase the sport for what the sport is genuinely good for: the development, the joy, the doors it can open, the human it builds. Just don't bet the college fund on an outcome with those odds. Run the net-cost math on every school. Compare the D3-with-merit-aid number against the D1-with-partial number honestly. And keep the athletic scholarship in its proper place — a possible bonus, never the foundation.

The families who understand this make calmer, smarter, cheaper decisions, and they stop sacrificing the present chasing a financial mirage. Athletic money should be the cherry on top. The cake is the transcript, the aid, and the fit.

The Eligibility Panic Trap The scholarship conversation now gets tangled with eligibility, roster caps, transfer movement, NIL, and social media panic. That makes the financial conversation even more important.

When rules feel uncertain, families often start spending to create a sense of control. Another event. Another advisor. Another academy. Another year. Another promise that this path will protect the athlete from whatever change is coming.

Be careful.

Uncertainty is expensive when fear is driving the purchase.

Before spending money because of a rule change or eligibility headline, ask whether the issue actually applies to your athlete, your sport, your level, your division, your timeline, and your family goals. Ask whether the rule is final or still being discussed. Ask whether the decision will improve the athlete's academic life, athletic development, family health, or long-term options.

If the only answer is, "We are afraid not to," pause.

The financial plan should not be built around panic. It should be built around the true net cost, the academic opportunity, the fit, the family values, and the life your athlete is trying to build.

Do not pay for certainty that no one can honestly sell.

Chapter Tool

(See full tool in the Parent Toolkit Appendix.)

Chapter 40: Sports as a Door, Not the Whole House

Helping Athletes Become More Than Their Sport

We arrive, at the end of this book, at the question that holds all the others: who is your child when the sport is gone?

Because the sport will be gone, for every athlete, eventually. For most, it ends in high school. For some, in college. For the rare few, after a professional career. But it ends for all of them, and the day it does, what's left is the person the sport helped build. That's the whole point of everything in these pages — and it's why the last and most important idea is this: let sport be a door into a bigger life. Never let it become the whole house.

The door and the house

A door is a wonderful thing. Sport opens doors an athlete couldn't open any other way — to discipline, to friendship, to confidence, to scholarships and schools and experiences, to lessons that shape a whole life. As a door, sport is one of the great gifts of a young life, and I'd never tell a family to love it any less.

But a door is meant to be walked through — into a bigger room, a fuller life on the other side. The danger comes when a family stops treating sport as the door and starts treating it as the entire house, the only room the athlete lives in, the single word on their nametag. Because when "athlete" is all an athlete is, then a cut, an injury, a benching, a bad season, or the simple arrival of the final whistle isn't a setback. It's an identity collapse. There's no other room to stand in.

I've seen it: the athlete whose whole self was the sport, who got hurt or got cut or just aged out, and didn't know who they were anymore. That's not a sports tragedy. That's a parenting outcome we can prevent — by making sure, all along the way, that the athlete was always more than one thing.

I have also seen the opposite, and Riley Hebert is one of the people I think about. Riley was a Louisiana athlete who didn't have the college options he wanted coming out of high school. A postgraduate year at Salisbury, a boarding school in Connecticut, could have sounded from a distance like a baseball detour. But it became a doorway.

I'll never forget how it started. Riley's father, Ronnie, told me his son came home from a conversation about the opportunity so lit up that he couldn't sleep — three nights in a row. This kid has a fire in his belly, Ronnie said. How do I not put that out? A grandmother helped find the tuition. And a Louisiana kid who'd lived a mile from the LSU stadium got on a plane to a Connecticut winter.

It was not easy. Those first months were hard — no car, can't leave, all boys, a long way from home. Early on, his coach, John Toffey, sat him down and said something Riley still repeats: Burn the boats. You've made the decision to come up here. Lean in, give me your best, and you'll look back on this with fond memories. Then the New England winter arrived, and one day Riley called home and said, Dad, right field's covered in snow. Ronnie thought about driving up with a stack of snow shovels.

He burned the boats. Salisbury gave him more than another season — academic rigor, structure, time management, teachers and coaches who invested in him, and a network he's still using a decade later. It led to Division I baseball at UIC. And even there, the sport didn't hand him what he'd pictured: injuries cost him most of two years, and he never became the on-field star he'd imagined. But he became something that lasts longer — a captain, a culture-carrier, a young man who learned to lead when the game wouldn't give him the role he wanted. Then came Chicago, a marriage, a church community, a career across healthcare and finance, an MBA at Northwestern.

Years later, looking back on all of it, Riley said it better than I ever could: baseball was never the point. It was a horse the family chose to saddle up and ride — and it carried him somewhere far bigger than a ballfield. That is sport as a door. The game opened it. The life on the other side was always the real story.

How you keep the house bigger than the sport

You protect against it the same way you protect everything else in this book: with what you pay attention to and what you say. A parent whose face doesn't change with the scoreboard. Dinner conversations that aren't all about the game. Interests, friends, and a self that exist outside the lines. Asking "who are you" at least as often as "how'd you play." Making sure there are days when the athlete isn't being evaluated, measured, filmed, or compared — days when they're simply loved.

It means introducing your athlete as your son or daughter, not only as your athlete. It means noticing their kindness, their humor, their curiosity, their courage off the field as loudly as you notice their performance on it. It means modeling, as the adult, that you're a fan of the person, not just the player. Every one of those choices quietly builds rooms in the house beyond the one with the trophies — so that when the sport eventually leaves, the athlete is still fully at home in their own life.

What the sport was always for

Tie it back to the 40-year plan, because this is where the whole book lands. If the sport did its job, your athlete walks away from it — whenever that day comes — with everything that actually lasts: the discipline, the resilience, the friendships, the relationship with their own body, the knowledge that they can do hard things, the lessons learned from losing and getting back up. Sport will have been a magnificent door into all of that. And your athlete will walk through it into a life that's so much bigger than any game.

That's success. Not the trophy, not the ranking, not even the scholarship. Success is a whole, healthy, capable adult who happened to play a sport, walking through the door the sport opened into a full and meaningful life — and looking back on the whole thing with joy, not damage.

So love the sport for what it is: one of the best doors your child will ever walk through. Just never let it become the room they get stuck in. Let it open the door. Then let them walk through, into everything else they're going to be.

Because excellence was always the goal — but your child was always the point.

Chapter Tool

(See full tool in the Parent Toolkit Appendix.)

The Parent's Final Reset If this book has done its job, you should feel steadier.

Not because the youth sports world became simpler. It has not. There will still be teams, rankings, travel schedules, showcases, camps, clinics, trainers, group chats, social media posts, and other families making different decisions.

The difference is that you now have a framework.

You can pause.
You can ask better questions.

You can decide from wisdom instead of fear.

You can protect childhood and still support ambition.

You can build a serious athlete without turning the family into a business plan.

You can say no.

You can let your athlete own the dream.

You can keep the long game in focus.

Before every season and every expensive decision, return to the same promise:

I will not let fear make the plan.

Build the athlete.

Protect the joy.

Appendix: The Beyond the Bleachers Parent Toolkit

This toolkit gives parents practical filters, scripts, and worksheets to use before a season, after a hard game, before paying for an opportunity, before contacting a coach, and before making a major sports decision.

A. Parent Mindset Tools

The Parent Pledge

Beyond the Bleachers: I will not let fear make the plan.

I will support my athlete, protect our family, and keep the long game in focus.

I promise my love is not attached to the scoreboard. I will not change between great games and hard ones.

I will give my athlete the car ride home. It is theirs, not a review.

I will protect sleep, health, childhood, and the right to be a whole person who is more than an athlete.

I will choose fit over fear, development over exposure, and joy over my anxiety.

I will let the dream belong to the athlete.

Excellence is the goal, but the athlete is the point.

Parent: _____

Athlete: _____

Date: _____

The Parent Pause Rule

Before saying yes to another team, trainer, camp, showcase, ranking event, lesson, academy, or travel commitment, pause.

Ask: Am I making this decision from wisdom, or from fear?

Pause when the athlete did not ask for it, the family is exhausted, the cost creates pressure, joy is fading, another family is driving the decision, the opportunity promises exposure but cannot explain development, or the schedule leaves no room for rest, school, siblings, sleep, or childhood.

If two or more are true, the answer may be: not yet.

Not yet is a complete sentence.

The Fear-Purchase Gut Check

Am I buying my athlete an opportunity, or am I buying myself relief?

Opportunity has readiness, real evaluators, right timing, verified attendance, realistic fit, and clear purpose.

Relief sounds like: everyone else is going, vague promises, closing-door pressure, no verified evaluator list, no development, and parent anxiety driving the decision.

B. Age and Development Tools

Age 6-17 Development Roadmap

Ages 6-9: Fun, fundamentals, movement, confidence, local play, friendships, and trying without fear.

Ages 10-12: Organic repetition, healthy competition, simple instruction, multi-sport play, and progression-based coaching.

Ages 13-14: Puberty, comparison, nutrition, sleep, recovery, safe strength training, journaling, confidence, and patience.

Ages 15-17: Ownership, accountability, academics, communication, strength, recovery, body language, character, fit, and raising the floor.

Ages 10-16: Prepare, Don't Panic Roadmap

Ages 10-12: Build the athlete. Fun, foundation, fundamentals, repetition, play, confidence.

Ages 12-14: Grow through the middle. Maturity, learning style, travel-program fit, playing up when appropriate, and avoiding over-specialization.

Ages 14-16: Prepare. Strength, execution, competition, sport IQ, recovery, mental discipline.

Parent reset: Ages 10-16 are a preparation window, not a recruiting emergency.

The Compete / Execute / Workload Check

Before worrying about recruiting, ask:

1. Can my athlete compete against stronger athletes?

2. Can my athlete execute repeatable skills under pressure?

3. Can my athlete carry the workload physically, mentally, academically, and emotionally?

If these are not green checks, recruiting is not the priority yet.

Athlete Ownership Journal

Use once a week: one thing I did well; one thing I need to improve; one habit I will own this week.

C. Choices, Voices, and Program Evaluation Tools

The Choices and Voices Filter

Before letting any coach, trainer, advisor, program, online instructor, or evaluator become a voice in your athlete's life, ask:

1. Are they helping my athlete think, adjust, and own the work?

2. Are they making my athlete more confident or more confused?

3. Are they creating clarity, or selling urgency?

Final question: Is this voice helping us unplug from fear — or plug into more of it?

The Progression vs. Perfection Filter

Before paying for lessons or technical instruction, ask whether the coach teaches progression, uses simple language, and protects confidence while correcting skill.

If a young athlete leaves every lesson feeling broken, the instruction may be too much, too soon.

Coach Green Flags vs. Red Flags

Green flags: demanding and warm, teaches the why, develops the whole roster, honest without overselling, consistent with communication, safe with boundaries.

Red flags: shame disguised as toughness, fear-based motivation, favoritism, scholarship guarantees, no questions allowed, overuse pressure, one-size-fits-all instruction.

The test: A great coach makes your athlete braver. A bad coach makes your athlete more afraid.

Program Evaluation Checklist

[ ] Can they clearly explain their development philosophy?

[ ] Is playing time decided fairly, especially at younger ages?

[ ] Do they communicate expectations clearly?

[ ] Does the schedule leave room for school, sleep, siblings, and family?

Safeguarding and Safety Check

[ ] Are coaches background checked?

[ ] Are there clear supervision policies?

[ ] Are there rules around one-on-one communication and private spaces?

[ ] Is there a clear process for reporting concerns?

D. Health, Body, and Recovery Tools

Healthy Athlete Checklist

[ ] The athlete still wants to go.

[ ] The athlete bounces back from hard games.

[ ] The athlete is sleeping enough.

[ ] The athlete is eating enough.

[ ] The athlete is not chronically hurt.

[ ] The athlete still smiles, laughs, or lights up around the sport.

Burnout Warning Signs Checklist

Watch for patterns over two to three weeks: flat joy, dragging before practice, silence around the sport, sleep changes, appetite changes, irritability, anxiety, isolation, or loss of interest beyond sport.

Several signs mean slow down and start a calm conversation. Persistent concerns deserve qualified professional help.

Build the Body, Don't Judge the Body

Use building language: "Strong is the goal," "Let's fuel the work," "Your body is on its own clock," and "What do you need to feel ready?"

Avoid judging language: "You need to look more athletic," "You are behind," "Watch what you eat," or comparing the athlete's body to someone else's.

Arm Care Common-Sense Check

For throwing athletes, ask whether they play enough catch, move their feet when throwing, learn good recovery habits, and avoid confusing more throwing with better development.

E. Social Media, Rankings, Exposure, and Recruiting Tools

When Your Athlete Becomes Content — Parent Awareness Check

Before posting, streaming, tagging, or turning a performance into public content, ask whether this helps the athlete or feeds the parent's anxiety.

Rankings Reality Card

A ranking is a snapshot sold as a verdict. It is one frame of a moving picture. It is often wrong. It is always temporary. The best response is to return to the work.

Is This Real Exposure? Filter

1. Is my athlete actually ready to be evaluated?

2. Is my athlete at a stage where this matters?

3. Have we checked the evaluator list, rules, timing, cost, and fit?

Vague answers usually mean you are buying a weekend, not exposure.

Recruitability Reality Check

Ability: Does my athlete have a skill, tool, or trait that translates?

Academics: Does the transcript create options?

Character: Does the athlete handle teammates, coaches, and adversity well?

Coachability: Does the athlete listen, adjust, and apply feedback?

Ownership: Does the athlete communicate, manage routines, and take responsibility?

The Unbiased Evaluation Filter

Before accepting an evaluation, ask whether the evaluator is also selling lessons, a team, a showcase, or a program. Be honest about the conflict.

F. Parent-Coach Communication Tools

Coach Beede Car Ride Rule

The car ride home belongs to the athlete, not the coach.

Opening line, win or lose: I love watching you play.

Then let them lead.

If they want to talk, ask: Do you want me to just listen, or do you want my take?

Never say: What happened out there? Why didn't you? Do you know what this costs? You embarrassed yourself. You did not look like you wanted it.

Advocacy vs. Interference

Advocacy protects the person: safety, health, fair treatment, development.

Interference controls the outcome: minutes, position, lineup, tactics, comparison.

Advocacy asks questions. Interference makes demands.

The 24-Hour Rule Card

Praise can be immediate. Concerns wait 24 hours.

If it still matters tomorrow, raise it calmly. If it is gone by morning, let it go.

Stay or Go — The One Question

Are we leaving to escape adversity, or to escape harm?

Adversity can build. Harm damages.

Stay for healthy challenge. Leave unsafe or damaging environments.

G. Academics, Fit, and Long-Game Tools

Reclassification / Redshirt Decision Filter

Before repeating a grade, delaying graduation, taking a gap year, changing schools, or choosing a post-grad path, ask whether you are buying development time or anxiety time.

Final question: Are we buying development time, or anxiety time?

The Eligibility Panic Filter

Before reacting to an NCAA rule change, recruiting headline, social media post, or eligibility rumor, ask whether the rule is final, whether it applies to your athlete, and whether it changes the actual work in front of you.

Final question: Are we protecting the path, or reacting to panic?

40-Year Plan Gut Check

If the sport ended tomorrow, what would this build that my athlete gets to keep?

Does this serve the forty-year-old, or just this season?

Is sports still a door into a bigger life, or has it become the whole house?

Academic-Athletic Balance Check

[ ] Is schoolwork improving, holding steady, or slipping?

[ ] Is the athlete managing deadlines?

[ ] Is the sport supporting discipline, or becoming an excuse to avoid school accountability?

Fit-Before-Level Filter

Academic fit. Financial fit. Culture fit. Environment fit. Playing fit. Level last.

If level is the first question, you may be shopping for ego. Make it the last.

Scholarship Reality Worksheet

For every school, compare: total cost of attendance, athletic aid, academic/merit aid, need-based aid, travel cost, likely playing fit, academic fit, and long-term value.

Do not compare offers by label. Compare the real net cost and the full fit.

Final Parent Reset

I will not let fear make the plan.

I will choose fit over fear.

I will choose development over exposure.

I will choose wisdom over urgency.

I will choose the athlete over the schedule.

I will choose the family over the machine.

I will remember that childhood is not a race.

Build the athlete.

Protect the joy.